GIRAFFE JUICE

THE MAGIC OF MAKING LIFE WONDERFUL

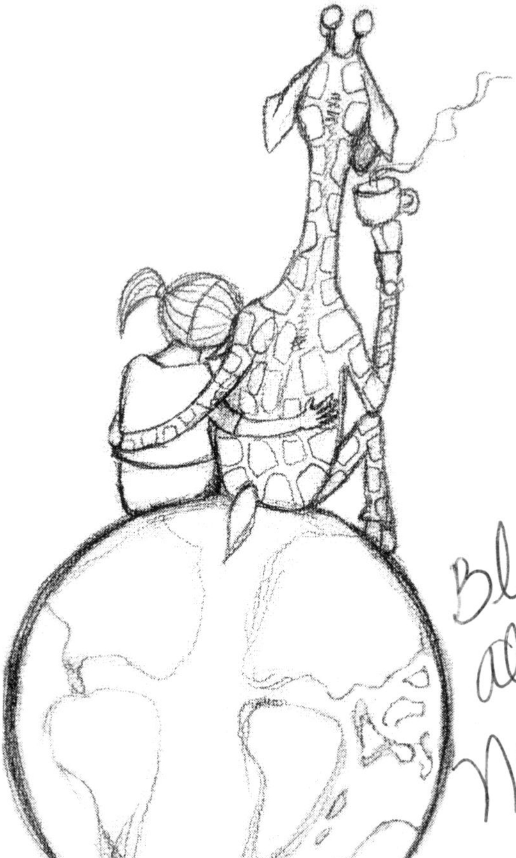

Blessings always, Marci

OTHER WORKS FROM THE AUTHORS

FUN HARMONICA LESSONS

JP OFFERS FREE ONLINE LESSONS FOR KIDS AND ADULTS

I would love to show you how to put a little ol' harmonica up to your mouth and blow the roof off the house! If you're willing to give it a try, I'm optimistic you can easily learn to inspire others…and play for your own enjoyment in less than a few hours (if you want to). You can instantly receive lots of free audio and video instruction by visiting me at **www.KidsHarmonica.com** and **www.Harmonica.com/nvc**. If you've never played a musical instrument before, harmonica is one of the world's easiest instruments for adults and kids to enter into the magical world of making music. Music communicates through all cultural borders. And once people are in communication…Peace is not far off…

A WONDERFUL FILM FOR KIDS

Marci directed **Sweetwater**: A kids' film aired by PBS that shares how family, friendship, and a spiritual connection to life can support people of all ages to make the best of challenging times. Go to **www.Sweetwaterfilm.com** to purchase the DVD.

YOGA FOR SENIORS

Marci created **Yoga For Seniors** to specifically meet the needs of senior citizens and people who are physically challenged. This gentle routine can be completed in less than thirty minutes. It is designed to strengthen the immune system, improve balance, mental clarity and peace of mind. Contact Marci at marci@GiraffeJuice.com to purchase the DVD.

MEDITATION CD

Clear Calm is a meditation CD with nature sounds and gentle clear instruction to remove stress. Gentle neck releases, Chi Quong (Chinese yoga) and yogic breathing exercises soothe the soul. Contact Marci at marci@GiraffeJuice.com to purchase the CD.

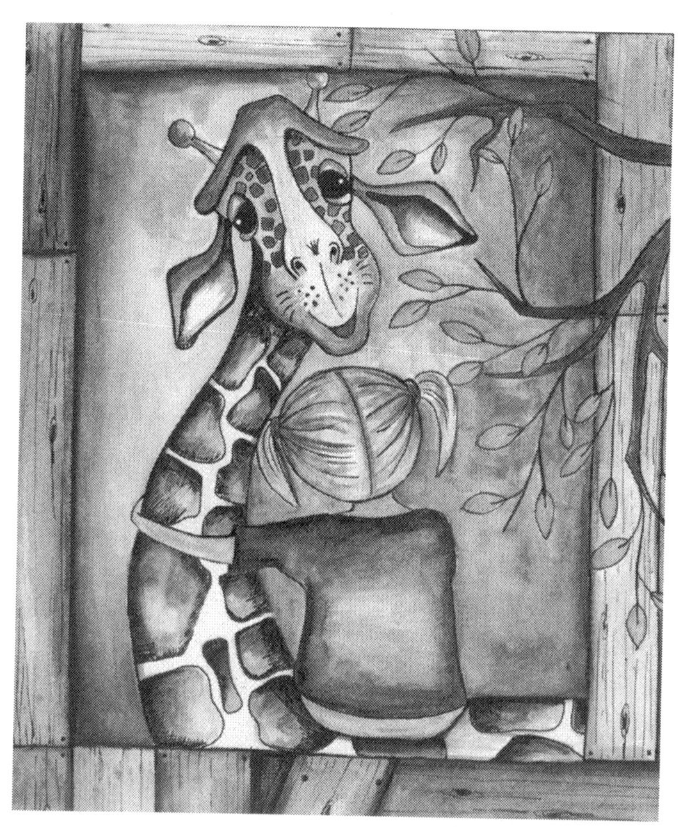

GIRAFFE JUICE

THE MAGIC OF MAKING LIFE WONDERFUL

MARCI WINTERS AND JP ALLEN
ILLUSTRATIONS BY TAMARA LAPORTE

Follow Your Joy Press

Published by:

Follow Your Joy Press
PO Box 208
Anahola, HI USA 96703

This book is manufactured in the United States of America.
Cover and interior illustrations by Tamara Laporte
Book design by Tania Wolk, Go Giraffe Go Writing & Design Inc.

ISBN:978-0-615-26393-9

WELCOME

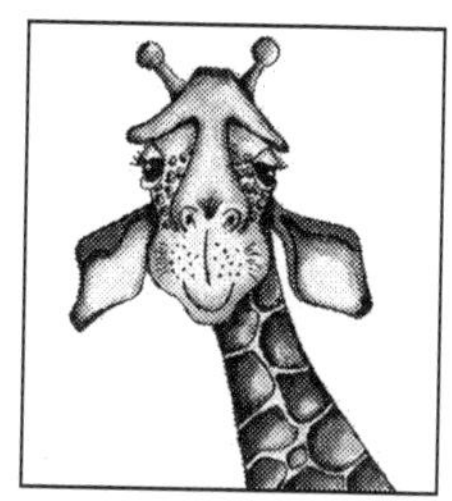

Hi there! My name is Marvel and I'm the giraffe in the story you're about to read. I'm so happy you're choosing to check out this book because I wrote it for you...well...for you and for everyone.

I'm pretty sure you're a human...since humans are usually the ones who read books. Perhaps you're thinking, Giraffes don't talk!? Well... we don't' talk the way people talk, but we do have our own special way of understanding each other...it's the reason we've been able to survive on the planet for thousands and thousands of years. Just like people, if we didn't know how to communicate we wouldn't be able to survive.

I just wanted to let you know before we start, you can give this story to anyone you want for free. When you go to GiraffeJuice.com I'll show you how to pass on the eBook in less than a minute.

Another cool thing you might enjoy is the Giraffe Juice Games Book that goes with this story. If you want to check it out you can download the eBook version for free at GiraffeJuice.com. There's more about this at the back of this book.

I hope you have a great time reading this book and it helps you remember the amazing power you have to make life fun.

Your Giraffe Buddy,
Marvel

~ 1 ~
BARELY BALANCED

Wow! A magical crystal wonderland, thought twelve-year-old Eva Cassidy. From the warm coziness of her bed, she was delighted to discover that the frosty night air had transformed the grass in her backyard into a glittering fantasyland. It was an unusually cold spring morning in the countryside of Fairtown, South Carolina, and the freckle-faced strawberry blond emerged from the cocoon of her comfy covers. She felt an exciting feeling in her bones that something special was going to happen today.

As she gazed around her bedroom, her eyes embraced one of her favorite companions in the whole wide world—her electric guitar, Blue Shine (that's the nickname she gave her guitar because of its metallic blue color). Eva played left-handed, which is pretty rare, so her dad secretly had it handmade for her, and surprised her with it on her birthday. Blue Shine was leaning against the wall and she imagined it reaching out to her and inviting her to play.

Eva whispered to her special friend, "Don't worry Blue Shine, you and I will have time to jam right after school."

Eva jumped out of bed and noticed her big purple peace-sign sweatshirt peeking out from her bottom dresser drawer. *Perfect*, she thought. She pulled the oversized, colorful warmth over her head, stuffed her harmonica in her pocket, and followed her stomach downstairs for breakfast.

Eva tiptoed down the stairs very quietly because she remembered that her mom had been up late baking Easter cookies. Knowing that the last step creaked loudly, Eva jumped over it and unexpectedly landed right on her brother's skateboard that was left out overnight. The next thing she knew it was too late. *OH NO*! Eva was hauling full-speed on an unexpected early-morning ride into the kitchen.

Barely balanced on the board, she went sailing headfirst into the fruit basket on the breakfast table.

—WHAP!—

Apples and oranges flew everywhere. She went tumbling with the peaches...smashed to the ground. *I'm in trouble now!*

Eva held her breath and froze, awaiting the groans and grumbles of her mom and dad upstairs. Her cat, Pumpkin, ran and hid in the corner. Neither of them moved. But to Eva's surprise, her parents didn't wake up. *Whew! Thank goodness.* Her eleven-year-old brother Bo was going to hear about this and it wasn't going to be pretty.

Eva cleaned up the floor, fed Pumpkin, and then she munched down two big bowls of cereal with fresh organic strawberries. Eva thought to herself, *I wonder where I can find an egg carton to plant some seeds for my science project? I'll bet there's one in the old barn out back. Dad loves to put old, used cans and bottles and things out there to be recycled.*

She quickly rinsed off her cereal bowl, put it in the dishwasher and scurried out the back door to explore.

Running down the big, steep hill in her backyard, she joyfully jumped over Bo's BMX bike ramp and did a spread eagle with her arms and legs reaching out into the air. *Yippie!*

She finally made it to dad's barn, which sat at the far corner of her big backyard. It was tucked away on the edge of a pine tree forest and there were no neighbors for miles. Dad had changed the tall barn into a workshop last summer, but lately he never used it because he was too busy at work.

Feeling afraid to enter the darkness of the barn, Eva paused as she approached the doorway. The air smelled musty. She stepped over some stinky gasoline cans and lots of rusty old tools. All of the strange smells gave her the creeps.

She thought about returning to the safety of home, but something called her to enter…she knew there were treasures to be found. Little did she know the unexpected treasure she would find that spring morning.

~ 2 ~
AN UNEXPECTED GUEST

Eva heard a lonely cry. "Meow..."

That doesn't sound like Pumpkin, she thought. Plus, Eva had let her cat into the house to eat breakfast.

"Meow," she heard again, followed by an abrupt **CRASH!**

BOOM!

BAM!

What was that? Eva was startled and on the verge of running, but what she saw next stopped her in her tracks. Towering over her was...it couldn't be...a giraffe? With a lampshade on its head...and meowing? *Giraffes don't meow.*

No way! This isn't happening. I must be dreaming. She blinked hard, trying to clear the sleep from her eyes. It was for real! There was a giraffe in dad's workshop...and he was big—really big. He wasn't full-grown, but he was clearly no baby. He was sort of tall and lanky, like a teenage giraffe.

Eva's mind was racing. *What is he doing here? And what's up with that dusty old lampshade on his head? Is he trying to hide? Yeah, right!*

The giraffe began backing into the corner. His long, bony legs bent and stretched awkwardly, looking like they could get tangled up at any moment. Clumsily, he managed to make it to the wall, where he tucked himself into a corner. Eva got the feeling he was really scared.

"Hi...uh...hi," the giraffe spoke, stuttering softly. "My...my name is..."

Eva fell over backward onto a bale of hay. *What's going on here? A talking giraffe? My brother must be playing a trick on me. Where are the video cameras?!*

"I'm lost," the giraffe said. "Would you help me find my mother? I'm scared."

Eva squeezed the harmonica in her pocket nervously, still not sure what was happening.

The giraffe looked really weird with the lampshade on its head. The silk string tassels that hung from the rim of the lampshade looked like windshield wipers as they swung from side to side over the giraffe's eyes. In spite of herself, Eva began laughing. The lampshade tumbled to the ground.

"Actually, I'm, um..." the giraffe said, "I'm out looking for my mom. She was transferred to a different zoo and I really miss her. I'm lost, and I'm not sure what to do."

Eva heard the fear and sadness in the giraffe's voice. She took a deep breath. "What was your name? I'm Eva."

"Well, my mom gave me the name Marshall..." he said, allowing his lengthy legs to take a few steps away from the corner, "...but everyone calls me Marvel because I'm always marveling about how amazed I am by life."

Just a few paces and he was practically right in front of her. Looking down at Eva, he smiled from cheek to cheek showing his big giraffe teeth.

"I find myself wondering about almost everything Eva...even weird things like why this dog I know won't eat green Jell-O. Even now I'm wondering something…I'm wondering…what you're wondering about, Eva?"

"Well, I'm wondering what you're doing here and how you got here...Marvel? That's kind of a weird name, but it's kind of cool too…"

Eva released her tight grip on the harmonica in her pocket as she relaxed. "Gosh, the last thing I expected to find this morning was a talking giraffe in my backyard." The corners of her mouth rose in amusement.

"I've never met a talking giraffe before. Since when do giraffes talk?"

Marvel laughed, and as he did his long eyelashes fluttered. "Well, we talk in our own special way, but lots of people have forgotten how to listen. Mostly, only young people can hear me. I'm so happy you're listening."

Eva's eyes brightened.

"I am! And I think it would be fun to help you find your mom. Maybe we could break into the zoo and free her! And maybe you could both live here, and I could take care of you!"

Marvel took a deep breath and sighed, "I feel so relieved you want to help me." He closed his eyes and allowed his neck to rotate in a big, big circle.

"At the same time, Eva, I'm concerned that the people who run the zoo wouldn't be happy with our breaking in to get my mom. And even though sometimes I don't like living in a cage, I'm wondering if we can come up with a plan that works for the zoo people too."

Eva was surprised that Marvel cared so much about the zookeepers who kept him locked up in a cage.

Eva clenched her fists and changed the subject. "There's this bully at school named Jip Jackal who locked me in a closet last week at school. I hope he gets expelled."

Marvel's eyes became soft and his ears began to wiggle gently as he listened.

"He's always pushing me and pulling my hair," she said, crossing her arms over chest. "I've tried everything to make him stop, but he won't."

Marvel began swaying his long body from side to side as he adjusted his back legs. Suddenly, his back end dropped. He appeared to be sitting down. Eva wasn't sure if he had lost his balance, or had deliberately sat down.

"Well, Eva," Marvel's calm voice made her assume that he hadn't fallen. "Are you frustrated because you've tried really hard to get Jip to leave you alone?"

Eva looked up into his big giraffe eyes. They looked deep, like the sky at night. She smiled. "Yeah, that's right. Thanks for listening, Marvel…I…I just don't know what I ever did to Jip to make him want to be so mean to me. We used to be friends. He even told me once he was embarrassed about his real name—Jaypeeski. And I've always kept it a secret."

Marvel spoke gently. "Are you bummed because you're missing your friendship with Jip?"

"Yeah. I guess I feel sad because we actually used to have a lot of fun together."

Eva was surprised at how comfortable she felt sharing so much with Marvel. The way he listened and understood seemed to melt something inside of her. Her eyes welled up. "You know, I actually feel better seeing that I don't hate Jip; maybe I just miss being his friend."

Eva walked over and began petting Marvel's fur. "Jip and I used to hang out at the park and he'd act like a monkey and tell me funny jokes. We laughed so hard together." She smiled at the memory, but then suddenly her smile vanished. "Well, that was before he started hanging out with all his bully friends."

Eva looked down at the ground but then suddenly her eyes lit up. "Do you want us to be friends, Marvel? We could make a buddy pact—I'll show you how! Reach out your hoof."

Marvel's eyes twinkled as he put his hoof in Eva's hand. He was wearing a big watch with a grape-juice-colored wristband. Eva tilted her head, becoming aware of how strange it was to have a giraffe in her dad's barn that talked and was wearing a watch. She shook his hoof, performing the secret handshake she had learned from her best friend, Ike. The dawn's rays poured into the barn as the sunrise seemed to smile a giraffe orange that morning.

After the secret handshake ritual was complete, Eva suddenly realized she still didn't know the answer to an important question. "How did you get here anyway, Marvel?"

"Someone brought me here, but I'd rather not talk about it just yet because I don't want this person to get in trouble for trying to help me. Is that okay, Eva?"

"Sure." Eva got the feeling Jip Jackal might have something to do with it but she quickly changed the subject.

"Hey Marvel. Do you ever wonder why some people like to bully and other people like to be nice?"

Marvel paused and scratched his chin with his hoof. "You know Eva, I have wondered that...but I think about it a little differently. I listen to people talk from my cage at the zoo all day. Of course, they usually don't know that I can understand them," Marvel grinned and went on, "I've been trying to figure out why some people choose violence, when it seems to me that the thing people really love best is to make like fun and to take care of each other."

As he walked past the workbench, his front leg grazed a corner, and a loud clattering of tools startled him.

He jumped back, almost tripping over himself. Realizing that it was just the sound of tools, he relaxed. Marvel planted his legs and stood as still as a tree. Stillness appeared to be the best way to keep his big, lanky body from bumping into things.

He cleared his throat as if nothing had happened and just as he was about to speak, they both heard a roar. "Eva! Where are you? It's time for school!"

It was Eva's mom projecting her voice from the top of the hill with her hands cupped around her mouth.

Eva rolled her eyes. "Coming, Mom!" She quickly looked over to Marvel and whispered, "Will you keep this a secret for now—you know, our meeting here?"

"Okay," Marvel agreed. For now it was their secret. "Will you come back and meet me here after school, Eva?"

"Of course," she responded with excitement.

"One more thing, Eva, if it's possible, could you bring me some green tea and a cinnamon stick? My mom and I used to enjoy it together on special occasions. I find it calming."

Eva skipped backward away from Marvel, keeping her eye on her friend for as long as she could. Before she turned and blasted out the door, she called out, "Green tea and a cinnamon stick. Cool. I'll try to hook you up!"

As Eva ran full speed toward the house her heart was pounding. She promised herself that she wouldn't tell anyone about Marvel. If Jip Jackal got wind that she was talking to a giraffe, he'd probably tease her about it forever.

~ 3 ~
IN A PICKLE

As Eva walked through the big red doors of her school that day, she got a sour, sinking feeling in her stomach. It was Tuesday; gym class was first period. Jip Jackal would be there and he loved to pull on her pigtails.

Eva went into the girls' bathroom to splash some water on her face and calm down. She decided to comb the pigtails out of her hair. While gazing at herself in the big bathroom mirror, Eva began to wonder: *Maybe Jip would stop bothering me if I told him that I miss hanging out with him… No, he'd probably tell the other kids and they'd start laughing at me. I don't know what to do… I wish I could just stay home with Marvel.*

Who the heck brought him to the barn and left him there, anyway? And why is Marvel keeping it a secret? No matter what, I've got to help him find his mom before the people at the zoo catch up with him.

Suddenly, Eva heard the bell ring—she was late for first period! The moment she stepped out of the bathroom, she saw Principal Pickle at the end of the empty hallway, marching in her direction. Eva couldn't help but notice that he looked a lot like his last name, with slightly greenish, wrinkled skin. He had a stiff way of walking that inspired uncomfortable feelings in Eva. He always wore huge black leather shoes that looked almost like army boots.

His footsteps were approaching, getting louder with every stiff thump. Eva swallowed. "Oh no," she muttered to herself, wanting to duck back into the bathroom.

"Eva Cassidy, I consider you one of my best students. What are you doing out in the hall?"

"Um…uh…well…there's this kid," she said, feeling unsure of how to explain herself, "and, well, he's been bullying me…"

"Does your teacher know you're out here wandering around the hall?" Principal Pickle persisted.

"No," Eva confessed, dropping her head. She felt bummed that Principal Pickle didn't seem to care about the reason she was having a challenging day.

"Go to my office. You should know better."

"Okay," she said softly.

"We all go through challenges in our lives," Principal Pickle added before letting her go. "I was picked on as a kid, too, and I remember how hard it was. But in the long run it only made me stronger. You're too sensitive."

Eva felt sad and thought to herself, I wish Principal Pickle could just understand me instead of lecturing me and giving me his stupid advice. It would be so cool if Marvel could teach Principal Pickle how to listen like a giraffe.

When she got to the office, she saw Patty, the principal's secretary, talking on the phone. She was a tall, skinny woman with long, bony fingers and red, white, and blue striped fingernails. She was wearing funny old-fashioned glasses that looked like a cat's narrow eyes.

Patty whispered in an angry voice, "I've got to go," and then quickly hung up the phone. Eva got the feeling she was talking to her boyfriend and not working. Peering over her eyeglasses, Patty pointed to the bench outside of Principal Pickle's door.

Eva sat in a lump on the bench, playing with a black thread dangling from the big bottom button of her blue jeans.

Patty's high-pitched voice gave her goose bumps. Then more goose bumps popped up when Principal Pickle made his entrance.

"Come into my office, please, Ms. Cassidy."

Principal Pickle started the conversation with the obvious question: "Why were you in the hall without a pass, Eva?"

No answer would be good enough. He told her that she should have known the rules.

Eva felt ashamed and wished he could understand how anxious she felt inside, knowing that Jip Jackal would be there in gym class, waiting to torment her. Her mind was racing, and he kept preaching. His words all blurred together, and he ended with, "There will be no exceptions."

Finally, he let her go. He gave her a very serious warning and told her she would face detention if he heard of any other incidents. That was his word—"incidents." Her dad also used that word when he was mad. She felt sick to her stomach, and to make things worse, she was about to face Jip Jackal in gym class.

~ 4 ~
HAVING A BALL

When Eva got to the gym, the class was split up into groups. Four circles of kids were practicing soccer exercises. She stood at the doorway, and something in her gut told her not to enter. Eva felt afraid sometimes when she heard the gym teacher use her loud speaking voice.

Mrs. Strikes was an athletic woman with a stopwatch that dangled from her belt loop. Oddly, she wore two watches on her left wrist, just in case one stopped working. Mrs. Strikes paced rapidly around the room shouting, "Great job! Good effort!"

Eva didn't like the way she used compliments as a way of bossing everyone around like a military general. She thought Mrs. Strikes was ridiculously loud, and that

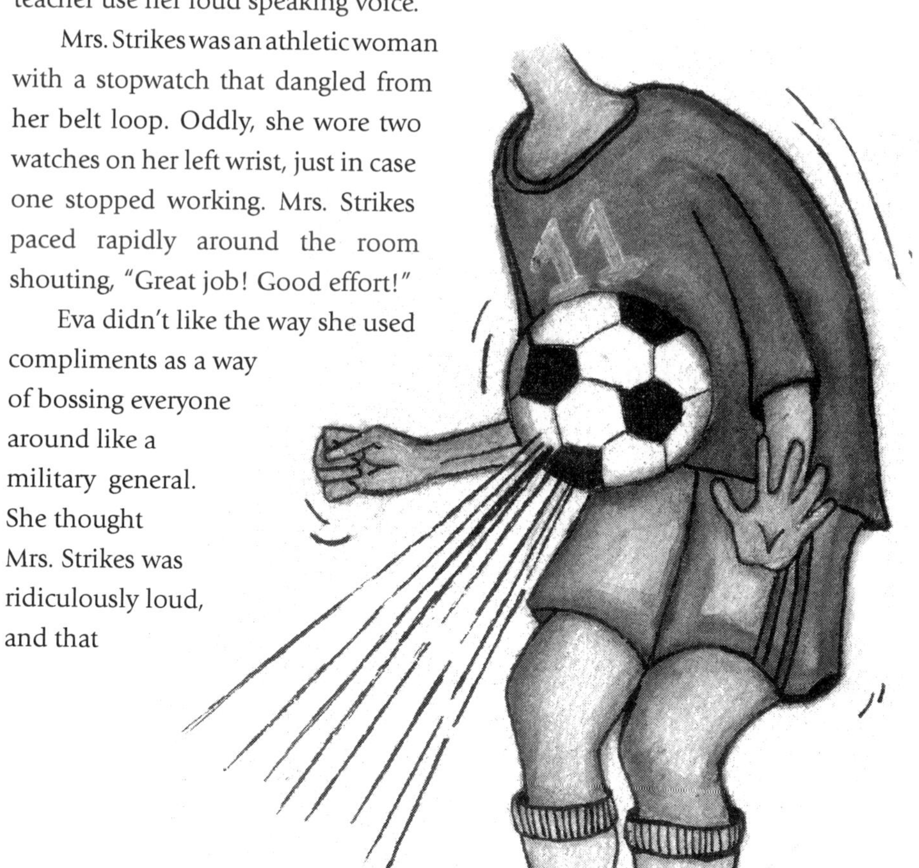

she favored Melissa Riley, who was the ultimate teacher's pet. The teachers all loved Melissa, because she got good grades. Mrs. Strikes always chose her to be goalie.

When Mrs. Strikes saw Eva she announced, "Eva, you're late! Please join Jip's group over there in the corner."

Eva mustered up her courage and whispered, "Would it be okay if I joined Ike's group? I don't want Jip to pick on me today."

Mrs. Strikes tried unsuccessfully to sweeten her voice. "Eva, if you hadn't come late to class, I could have put you in another group. Right now I'm requesting that you join Jip's group over there in the corner."

"Do I have to?" Eva asked, feeling choked up.

Mrs. Strikes took a step back and spoke with her lips pursed more tightly than usual. "If you don't want it to show up as a bad grade on your report card, you'll do as I requested."

Some request, Eva thought to herself. *I'd rather get a bad grade than have to deal with Jip. But I guess I don't have a choice. If I get a bad grade, my dad will take away my allowance, and then I won't be able to do stuff like go to the movies with my friends. I hate school.*

Eva put on a fake smile and walked over to Jip's group, hoping the other kids would be too busy kicking the soccer ball around to notice how much she was hurting inside.

"Look who decided to show up for class," Jip teased with a hungry look in his eyes.

"Leave me alone, Jip!" Eva said as her heart sped up and her face turned the color of a cranberry. She held her tightened fists by her sides, feeling cold sweat covering her hands.

Jip mimicked her, "Leave me alone!"

She could feel her anger building. Someone in the group passed the soccer ball to her, **and she kicked it as hard as she could into Jip's stomach, shouting, *"Bully!"***

Jip bent over, with the wind knocked out of him. Catching his breath, he sneered, "Oh, you want to play dirty!" Jip pulled his leg as far back as possible and then kicked the soccer ball smack into Eva's face.

Her left cheek stung like pins and needles. She held back her tears, because she didn't want the other kids to make fun of her.

"Now we're even!" Jip said, looking a little stunned himself. Then he smiled with a grin that declared victory. Two of the other boys began to laugh and slapped him a high-five. Of course, Mrs. Strikes didn't see a thing.

~ 5 ~
MAKING LIFE WONDERFUL

The three o'clock bell could not have rung soon enough. Outside, Eva eagerly gazed across the long line of waiting cars. She saw her mom's head peeking out from their brown boxy Volvo. Eva's dad had converted it to an electric car that didn't need gasoline by using a kit he bought online. It was quiet and fast, and Eva's friends thought it was cool that it didn't stink up the environment because it ran on water and solar power. Her mom waved and Eva got into the car.

"Hi, sweetie. How was your day?"

"It was okay." She decided not to tell her about the little trip to

Principal Pickle's office or her problem with Jip. "What are we having for dinner?" Eva's stomach rumbled. She also decided not to tell her mom that she was so upset she couldn't even eat her lunch that day.

"I think I'll make chicken. What do you think?"

Chicken sounded boring. She told her mom she wanted veggie burgers.

"Really? Veggie burgers?" her mom replied. In response, Eva's stomach growled, loudly enough that her mom heard it. "Alrighty, veggie burgers it is!"

Her mom pulled up to the curb to drop Eva off and then rushed off to buy groceries. Excited to see Marvel, Eva sped into the house and threw her backpack on the sofa.

Remembering that he'd asked for green tea with a cinnamon stick, she quickly made some in a big coffee mug and carefully carried it down the steep hill to the barn.

Eva whispered, "Marvel, are you here?"

"Over here, Eva!" Marvel spun his neck around and hit an aluminum ladder that was leaning up against the wall. Eva cringed as the ladder started falling in slow motion toward Marvel.

"Look out!"

Hearing Eva scream, Marvel jumped and almost got completely out of the way but the ladder came down on his front leg. Marvel let out a strange noise that started as a squeal and ended as a grunt, "YeeeeeUMPF!"

"Are you okay, Marvel?"

"Woof. That was a close call. That thing almost hit me right on the head. Thanks to you, I'm fine." Marvel immediately noticed the tea in Eva's hand. His eyebrows lifted with delight. She held out the mug, and he began to lick up the tea with his long purple tongue and flabby lips. "Yummm," he hummed like a Tibetan monk.

The sound of Marvel slurping and humming with pleasure was so funny to Eva that she had difficulty holding the mug steady.

When Marvel twisted up his tongue and grabbed the cinnamon stick, Eva could no longer contain herself. She started laughing so hard that the tea spilled all over the wooden floor and splattered onto their feet.

At this point, Marvel began to laugh as well, causing Eva to laugh even harder. Eva starting making that sound Marvel yelped when the ladder hit his leg, "YeeeeeUMPF! YeeeeeUMPF!"

This started a chain reaction of laughter that sent them both flying into a brand new space of joy. After three solid minutes of laughing, Eva's belly started to hurt and she couldn't bear it any more. She forced some long deep breaths to stop the laughter.

They looked at each other in silence for a moment and Marvel finally spoke up. "I'm so happy to see you, Eva. How was your day at school?"

"It stunk!" Eva exclaimed.

"I'm sure it wasn't as stinky as some of the baboon cages at my zoo," Marvel joked.

Eva cracked a smile and went on, "I really wanted to stay home from school, because I knew that Jip Jackal would be mean to me again." She scrunched her eyebrows as she remembered, "He's mean every day," and she threw her hands up in the air. "I wish there was some way for him to see it's just not cool. I mean, sometimes I think about going to another school just to get away from him…but I don't want to because I like my friends…and I like learning…but I can't focus lately."

Marvel's ears began to wiggle and he spoke softly. "Gosh, Eva. I can tell how hard this has been for you…seems like you're feeling pretty hopeless about getting along with Jip…so much so it's making it challenging to focus on learning…"

Eva let out a deep breath and her shoulders dropped. "Thanks Marvel. You know...even though I feel kind of bummed about what's been going on with Jip, it feels good to know that you understand me."

Eva looked curiously at Marvel. "I noticed something. When I was just telling you my problems, your ears started to wiggle. And then instead of giving me advice like most people do…you just listened and really tried to understand me…I really liked that, Marvel…I mean…sometimes I like people's advice but a lot of the time it's really annoying..."

Eva puffed out her cheeks. "One of the reasons I don't like to tell my dad things is because all he ever does is give me advice."

Marvel's ears started to wiggle. "Eva are you wishing that your dad would sometimes just listen to you and try to understand you instead of…"

Eva jumped in and interrupted him. "You're starting to do it again, Marvel. What is that? I mean...every time you wiggle your ears, you talk to me in a way that feels good. Will you tell me the secret to how you do that?"

A big smile came over Marvel's face. He kneeled down on his front legs and then leaned against the back wall of the barn to get comfortable. Eva snuggled up next to him and propped her head up on his belly. "Well...my secret. I'm glad you asked, Eva, because it's one of my favorite things. I like to call it the Giraffe Game. I'd love to share the secret of the Giraffe Game with you."

Marvel stretched out his front leg to get a bit more comfortable.

"Marvel!" Eva's eyes grew wide as she noticed blood on his leg. "What happened? Oh my gosh, you didn't tell me you were hurt! It must have been that ladder."

Marvel looked down at his leg. "Oh, it's just a little scratch."

"But it's bleeding," Eva said. She gently brushed away the hair around the cut to see how bad it was.

"How does it look?" Marvel finally asked.

"Well it must have gotten dirty when you kneeled on it. Can I help you clean it up?"

Eva jumped up and ran toward the door before Marvel got a chance to answer. "I'm getting a first-aid kit and then you can tell me about the Giraffe Game while I'm dressing your wound with a bandage." She called out as she was leaving the barn. "I'll be right back!"

~ 6 ~

A GAME WHERE EVERYONE WINS

"Okay, so you were about to tell me about the Giraffe Game," Eva said when she came back into the barn. She knelt before Marvel with the first-aid kit in her hand.

"Thank you." Marvel spoke tenderly as Eva took a wet towel and gently patted his cut. "Let's make believe, Eva, that each morning when you wake up, you can choose between two different games to play. One is called the Giraffe

Game; the other is called the Blame Game. The goal of the Blame Game is to decide who's right and who's wrong...who's good and who's bad...who's the winner and who's the loser."

Eva opened the first-aid kit and took out a few cotton balls while Marvel continued. "But the Giraffe Game is about finding a way for everyone to be a winner!" She poured out a little liquid onto the cotton and began to rub his cut. "Don't worry, Marvel, this stuff doesn't sting."

"Okay," Marvel nodded, but he closed his eyes anyway and waited for Eva to finish. When Eva was done cleaning his cut, he opened his eyes and went on.

"I like the Giraffe Game because it's kind of like being a detective. And the mystery I want to solve is: how can I find a way for everyone to be a winner..." Marvel blinked. His eyelashes were so long they reminded Eva of a fan made of peacock feathers. With a look of pure joy he huddled up close to Eva and whispered, "...even when sometimes it seems impossible for everyone to be a winner."

"Well it is impossible for everyone to be a winner sometimes, Marvel. Isn't it?" Eva asked with her hands up in the air, a big bandage dangling from her fingers. "Like in sports. There's a winning team and there's a losing team.

"I see what you're getting at, Eva. One thing to remember is that this is just a game. Life is usually not this simple. But..."

Marvel paused as Eva carefully pressed the bandage over his cut. "What if the losing team was expecting to be crushed by the first place champions, but they surprised themselves by taking the champions to triple over-time before they lost? The losers may walk off the court feeling like winners because they played better than they themselves or anyone ever expected."

Eva jumped in, "So even though they lost, they felt like winners. This is starting to make sense, but there's something I'm not getting. I mean...how do I learn to play the Giraffe Game? Can you just tell me the secret?"

"Well, you already know the secret, Eva...actually, I believe that everyone does. People sometimes just forget. Let's try this, Eva…" Marvel swatted a fly with his long tail. "Can you think of something that you did for someone that you really enjoyed?"

Eva finished tying the ends of the bandage and gently patted the spot over Marvel's wound to let him know she was finished. She gave a satisfied smile and then set his hoof back on the ground. Her face lit up.

"Oh, I know, Marvel. I loved bringing you the tea and cinnamon stick earlier!"

"And what did you love about it?"

"I loved to see you laugh, Marvel. And I loved the feeling I got when we were laughing together."

"So you love the feeling of making both of our lives wonderful at the same time."

"Oh, I see what you're getting at, Marvel. In the Giraffe Game we can both win!" Eva tapped the first-aid kit beside her and said, "Like when I tended to your cut, it made me happy knowing that I could help you with your wound. I think I get it," she nodded. "But you know, it isn't really a game, Marvel. It's more just a way to treat people."

"Yeah, I get what you're saying," Marvel agreed. "I just like to call it a game because it makes learning more fun. It also reminds me that life is rarely this simple and that there is really no right way to play the game. Everyone plays in their own unique way, but the goal remains the same...to find ways for everyone to win…even when it seems impossible. As I'm sure you know, Eva, there are a lot of challenges all over the planet right now. So it's very important to me to share the Giraffe Game with anyone who wants to learn."

Eva jumped up. "I want to learn! So how do I play the Giraffe Game?"

"You already did it—when you

GIRAFFES SAY:

Giraffes like to play the MAKING LIFE WONDERFUL GAME a whole lot more than the BLAME GAME. IN THE BLAME GAME THERE'S ALWAYS A LOSER. Giraffes love it when everyone wins.

gave me the tea and cinnamon stick, and when you cared for my injury. The tricky part is to be able to play the game with someone like Jip Jackal. It's sometimes challenging, even for me, to be able to open my heart and want to help people who scare me or do things I don't like. Now that's a tall order!"

"Not as tall as you!" Eva giggled as she stood on her tiptoes, reaching up to Marvel. "But seriously, I'm starting to wonder about something. I've never really thought about how I treat Jip…I just always think about how I don't like the way he treats me. I wonder if I change the way I treat him, he'll change the way he treats me?"

A sunbeam coming from the crack in the roof got brighter and beamed on Marvel's face. "I feel delighted hearing you say that, Eva. So, if you'd like to change the way you treat Jip, I can show you a shortcut for playing the Giraffe Game with someone who is hard for you to get along with."

"Sure. I love shortcuts. How does it work?" Eva reached up to hug Marvel and she tenderly petted the soft golden mane that grew along the back of his neck.

Marvel nuzzled closer and then licked a kiss across her forehead. *Yuck!*—his long purple tongue felt rough and weird.

GIRAFFES SAY:

Rather than being focused on always getting our own way, the goal of MAKING LIFE WONDERFUL is to give to one another in a way that feels fun, natural, and easy.

"Well, the shortcut has four simple steps that are easy to learn and they will help you learn fast."

Eva felt hopeful in some ways, but she also found it hard to believe she would ever be able to make friends with Jip Jackal.

She looked down at her watch. "Oh, gosh! It's time for dinner." She gave Marvel a quick hug, and a gentle kiss next to his bandage. "I'll come back with leftovers later," she assured him as she left the barn.

Marvel licked his lips. Eva planned to do her homework quickly and then come back to feed Marvel. Until she could find a way to get him back to his mom, she really liked taking care of him.

~ 7 ~
THE UNIVERSAL LANGUAGE OF PEACE

Eva was scared to break the news to her parents that a giraffe was living in the barn in their backyard. She thought to herself, *I really want to have some time alone with Marvel, and if I tell Mom and Dad, they'll probably call the zookeepers to take him away.*

So after dinner, Eva announced to her mom and dad that she had finished most of her homework and that she was going to practice her guitar in the barn. She secretly stuck a bag of sweet potatoes into the outer pocket of her guitar case and then snuck out the back door. When Eva arrived at the barn, she gave Marvel the bag of sweet potatoes and, before you could say *gobblin' greens,* Marvel wolfed down half the bag.

"YUMMMmmmm!"

Eva smiled, hearing the funny slobbering sounds Marvel made when he chewed. Upon finishing, Marvel looked at Eva with a satisfied grin. And just at the edge of that satisfied grin, Eva noticed a little dangling chunk of sweet potato.

"Come here, Marvel." Eva motioned him toward her with a wiggle of her forefinger. "You got something right here." She pointed to the corner of her own mouth, as if mirroring him.

Marvel carefully lowered his head and brought his face right up to Eva's. Her fingers gently brushed away the food. "Got it!" she said and then Marvel's head took the long journey back up toward the ceiling.

"Marvel," Eva said, sitting down on a small stool she had dragged over from her dad's workbench. "Can you tell me who brought you here to the barn? We're becoming such good friends, and it doesn't feel right that you're keeping a secret from me."

Marvel took a deep breath and his ears began to wiggle. "Eva, are you feeling uncomfortable because you want there to be trust in our friendship?"

Eva smiled inside, noticing that when Marvel listened carefully to her, his ears wiggled.

"Well, yeah, Marvel." She leaned forward on the stool with her elbows on her knees and her chin resting on her closed fists. "Thanks for understanding."

"You know, Eva, I want to make sure that the person who brought me here doesn't get in trouble. Is it okay with you if I wait to tell you until after you've finished learning the four steps of the Giraffe Game?

"I have a strong feeling that, once you understand how to use all four steps, you will feel much more powerful dealing with the tricky situations that may lay ahead of us."

"Okay, Marvel, that's cool I guess. But can we start now?" Eva asked, sitting up straight.

Marvel began. "Okay. Step one is to make an observation. What

I'd like you to do first is think of something specific that someone did—something you didn't enjoy. And, when you're ready, please tell me what that person did."

"Oh, that's easy," Eva responded without hesitation. "Jip Jackal bullied me at school today."

Marvel said calmly, "Can you see that when you say 'Jip bullied me at school today,' it doesn't really tell me exactly what he did? You are actually telling me your opinion."

"It's not just my opinion, Marvel." Eva threw her hands on her hips and pursed her lips. "Everyone at school knows that Jip is a bully, even Principal Pickle!"

"Now you're telling me what other people think about Jip. That still doesn't tell me what he specifically did. To make an observation, try saying exactly what happened, without mixing in any of your opinions about Jip."

Eva looked confused.

"I think this will help. Close your eyes and imagine you are watching a video of what happened today with Jip."

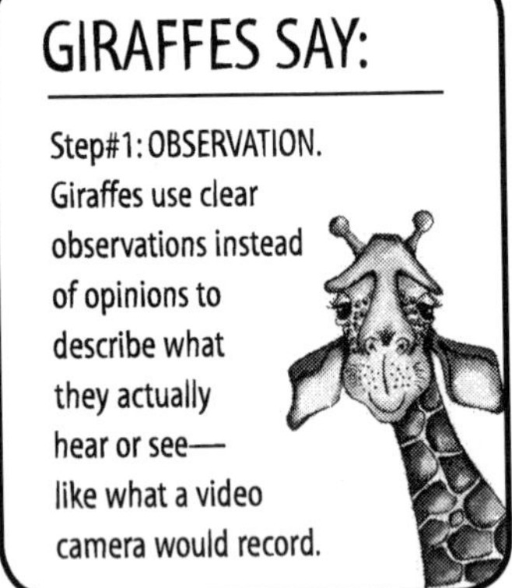

Eva closed her eyes.

"Now, describe what happened in your mental video, using words that every single person who watched the video could agree on—even Jip himself."

"Oh, I get it! That's easy. Jip kicked a soccer ball and it hit me in the face."

"Now we're cookin'! That's exactly what I'm looking for—an observation that's not mixed with your opinion. The idea is to say what happened in a way that makes it easier for the other person to hear the next three steps without starting an argument.

"Can you see how Jip might disagree if you told him that he

bullied you? Maybe he would say that you started it and he was just defending himself. If you get in an argument, you may get stuck on step one and you may never get a chance to do the next three steps... which is where it gets fun."

GIRAFFES SAY:

OBSERVATIONS instead of **OPINONS:** Giraffes are careful to not mix their opinions with their observations. (They get in a lot fewer arguments that way)

"Okay, I get it," Eva jumped in. "But it's so much easier to call him a bully…I even like to call him worse words than that," she smirked.

"Well, if you really want to call him a bully, be my guest, but just realize that you're playing the Blame Game. You're basically telling Jip that you think that you're the good guy and he's the bad guy. It's the same kind of thing people do when they go to war. They decide who the bad guys are and then try to take their power away and make them suffer.

"In the Giraffe Game, there are no good guys and bad guys because we want to find a way for everyone to win. I find that I get in fewer arguments when I use Giraffe Observations rather than opinions.

"So, guess what? We're already done with step one. Would you enjoy playing a song on your guitar as a way to celebrate?"

"Oh yeah, Marvel. And I'm ready to rip on some harmonica too!"

Eva barely went anywhere without her little pocket-sized friend. She loved bringing it to school because it was always hidden away in her pocket where no one knew. The guitar was too heavy to carry everywhere she went.

Eva didn't want the guitar and the harmonica to feel jealous of each other, so she figured out how to play them both at the same time. A special metal holder around her neck held the harmonica up to her mouth so she could keep her hands free for playing the guitar.

Eva imagined her harmonica and her guitar were two best friends that told each other musical stories. They sang to each other, they laughed together, and they even cried sometimes when they felt sad.

Eva slung her bright blue guitar over her shoulder and plugged it into her dad's old Fender amp that was stored in the barn. Then she moved her harmonica holder up to her mouth and started jamming.

First she played only the harmonica. It sounded like a train chuggin' down the tracks…faster…and faster. Marvel danced along, shaking his head from left to right with wild excitement. He was amazed at how she could make such an amazingly big sound out of such a little instrument.

When it seemed like there was no way for Eva to go any faster, she suddenly strummed her guitar without warning. The guitar roared loudly and took Marvel by surprise. He jumped back into the corner of the barn. His lanky legs just missed knocking over a garbage can.

Eva saw Marvel's face turn from fear to amazement as she played both the harmonica and the guitar at the same time…louder and faster…faster and louder…like a train screaming down the tracks. Eva screeched to a sudden moment of silence and then finished with a long, almost never-ending, high-pitched note.

She arched back, with one hand slapping the back of the harmonica and the other hand shaking the neck of the guitar to create a sweet, soulful, crying sound.

"WOOO WOOO WHEEEE!" Marvel squealed.

"That was fun," Eva giggled.

"You know," Marvel leaned his head down to Eva's level when he spoke, "I am sharing with you the way I speak because it may help you make life fun for yourself and others. But you already know another very special language that has an amazing power. Do you know what it is?"

Eva tilted her head and squinted her eyes. "English?" she asked. "That's the only language I know."

"Nope," Marvel chuckled, as he closed his eyes and shook his head.

A smile grew as he said, "I'm talking about music—I like to think of music as one of the universal languages of peace."

"What do you mean, Marvel?"

"Well, because everyone can understand music, it enables people to communicate even if they speak a different language...and once people start communicating, in whatever way they know how, it creates the possibility of ending violence and finding peaceful solutions."

Eva smiled and slowly strummed the guitar. "I've always felt that there was something special about music." She put her harmonica up to her lips and made a cool sounding bird call. "I like to take music with me wherever I go, and this harmonica makes it pretty easy!"

She played a slower song this time...a calm and peaceful song.

Marvel seemed to understand what she was trying to say with her song. He peacefully his closed eyes and nodded his head along with the music.

When the song ended, Eva set down her guitar and couldn't help but wrap her arms around Marvel, and he gently nuzzled his nose against her hair.

"Do you ever think there'll be peace on the planet Marvel? I mean...do you really think people will stop fighting wars?"

Marvel looked up at the ceiling as if he was looking for something... or maybe it was his giraffe way of praying. When he looked back down, there was a tear in his eye.

"I do believe that people will stop fighting wars someday, Eva, and here's why: I believe that whether they realize it or not, one of the things that people really love the most...something they love much, much more than fighting wars...is to make life wonderful for each other. And even though the world has a lot of problems right now, I have faith that people will soon come together very quickly and use their amazing creativity to improve life on earth for everyone."

Marvel began pacing the barn, slowly and carefully, especially when passing Eva's guitar that was delicately balanced against the wall of the barn.

"My giraffe ancestors have been on the planet for a long time, so we've seen how much human beings have changed over time. Most people don't know it, but humans have spent most of their time on Earth working together and living in peace. People have waged organized war on each other for only around ten thousand years. I know that seems like a long, long time, but it's really only a small percent of human history, Eva.

"Believe it or not, people lived without war for over one hundred thousand years. Considering this, I don't believe that humans are naturally violent; I just believe that they have gotten a bit confused and have forgotten that they like the Giraffe Game much more than violence.

"People have survived for all this time on the planet by working together and helping each other, so making life wonderful is something that everyone naturally knows how to do. It's just sometimes they forget and play the Blame Game instead."

There was a sparkle in Eva's eyes, and a sense of hope arose in her that she might even be able to get along with Jip Jackal some day.

"Okay, Marvel. I'm ready for the second step of the Giraffe Game. Do you want to start now?"

Marvel shouted playfully, with a thick Southern accent, "Bring it on!"

~ 8 ~
GIRAFFES HAVE FEELINGS, TOO

Eva took a look around the barn at the seemingly endless shelves that covered the walls. Upon them were toolboxes, old pairs of shoes, and many strange objects that Eva could not quite identify. She spotted a big mouse quickly scurry across the highest beam in the barn and disappear through a hole in the ceiling.

Looking at Marvel, Eva felt a sense of delight bubble up inside her. "I feel so happy. I don't know how you got here Marvel, but it's so cool that we get to spend this time alone together…hidden away in the barn where no one can find us."

Marvel's ears wiggled happily. He made a happy high-pitched noise that almost sounded like a horse:

"Yaaaaa HaHaHa!"

"Do you want to do step two now, Marvel?"

Marvel sang out, "Let's get this party started!" He then shook his hips and sent his tail flying from side to side. "Step two is all about feelings. It will help us get started if you answer the question, how did you feel when Jip kicked the soccer ball and it hit you in the face?"

GIRAFFES SAY:

Step #2: FEELINGS
When Giraffes talk about their feelings, they speak about themselves only, and no one else.

"I felt that what he did was wrong," Eva spoke, with her chin held high. "He shouldn't pick on girls."

"I'm glad you're playing along with me, but that's the Blame Game. In the Giraffe Game, I don't let myself get distracted with trying to figure out who's right and who's wrong. I try to stay very focused on caring about everyone and finding ways for each person to experience a sense of respect and fairness. Besides you used the Giraffe curse word that starts with an 's' and that's a sure sign that you're playing the Blame Game."

"What are you talking about Marvel?!" Eva scrunched up her nose. "I didn't use the curse word that starts with an 's'."

Marvel playfully bumped Eva's shoulder with the side of his head to make sure she knew that he was just having fun with her. Eva played along by getting in a karate stance with her arms held up like a boxer. Suddenly, without warning, she quickly reached out and squeezed Marvel's snout.

"You got me!" Marvel said as he lifted his head higher than she could reach and peacefully continued with a calm voice.

"When you said 'he shouldn't pick on girls,' you said the Giraffe curse word that starts with an 's'. Do you know which word I'm talking about?"

"Shouldn't?! That's not a curse word."

"In Giraffe Language, both should and shouldn't are curse words, because they're often used as part of the Blame Game. When you use these words, it's very possible that others will hear that they are being made wrong. "How do you feel when your teacher or your parents are angry and they use these words like this?

'You're just a kid so you should listen to your elders.'

'You shouldn't be so immature.'"

Marvel made a tick-tocking motion with his head—left to right, right to left—as he announced each command:

"You should know better than that.

You should clean your room.

You shouldn't eat so much candy.

You should go to bed.

You should be nicer to your brother.

'You should study and stop being so lazy.'"

GIRAFFES SAY:

Giraffes prefer not to use the words should and shouldn't. Sometimes when we use these words others may hear that they are being judged as "wrong."

"How do you like it when people use the 's' words with you?"

"I can't stand it!" Eva shuddered.

"After learning the four steps of the Giraffe Game, you'll see that there's a way to tell people like Jip Jackal what you want and what you don't want, without using the words 'should' and 'shouldn't.'"

Marvel quickly flicked his ear to shoo away a fly. "Would you like to try again, Eva? How did you feel when Jip kicked the soccer ball and it hit you in the face? This time try to share the feeling that's actually inside you, instead of what you're thinking."

Eva was stumped. "I don't really get it, Marvel."

"Maybe this will help: Any time you use words that involve another person, it's a thought and not a Giraffe Feeling. Feelings have a certain quality of energy…they are emotions that you can really feel inside of you—like joy, fear, or sadness."

GIRAFFES SAY:

FEELINGS instead of THOUGHTS: Giraffes know the difference between thoughts and feelings, and they are careful not to mix them up.

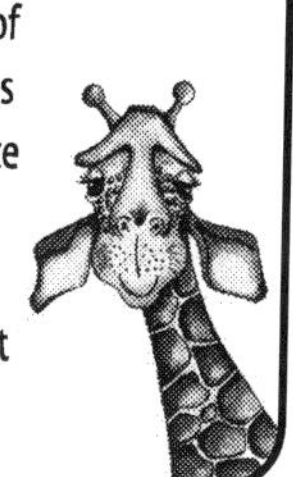

Eva's eyes widened. "I think I get it. Like if I say, 'I feel bullied,'

it's not a Giraffe Feeling, because it takes another person to bully me. You're wanting me to talk only about the feeling of the emotion I have inside myself."

"That's it, Eva. So, how did you feel when Jip kicked the soccer ball and it hit you in the face?"

Eva closed her eyes, took a deep breath, and pictured herself back at the scene. "I guess I felt embarrassed."

"There you go. You got it! We just finished step two! To review, step one is to make an observation, and step two is share the feeling that is inside of you. Only two more steps to go!"

Eva felt happy and proud. For a moment, she stopped thinking of Jip and noticed how odd Marvel looked there in Dad's barn. Suddenly, a twinge of sadness came over her, thinking about Marvel being separated from his mom.

"Eva?" Marvel could tell that her heart was somewhere else. "Are you okay?"

"Hmm..." She thought for a moment. "Well, I know we're on a roll with the four steps and everything, but I was thinking about how hard it must be for you to be separated from your mom. I really want to figure out a plan to help you get back together with her. What do you say, Marvel? Do you want to put our heads together?"

"I'm pretty sure that, if you want to help me reconnect with my mother, you're going to have to talk to the zookeepers, who are all adults. I feel optimistic that adults in general will take you more seriously if you first know how to speak Giraffe Language. Adults will be more likely to want to care about you, if you know how to communicate in a way that lets them know you also care about them."

Eva felt sad and became quiet. She stared at the ground, thinking to herself, *grown-ups have been bossing me around my whole life.* She wanted adults to take her more seriously, and it was hard to believe that Marvel's Giraffe Language could possibly help. At the moment she didn't feel like talking about it.

"You know what, Marvel? I know we only have two more steps to go, but I'm feeling kind of tired, and I have some homework to finish.

Do you think you could show me steps three and four tomorrow, after school?"

Marvel looked deeply into Eva's eyes and stood quietly. She got the feeling that he understood her sadness without having to say a word.

"Eva? How about you play a short song before you go?"

"Sure, Marvel." She pulled her harmonica from her pocket.

She decided to play a new song she had just learned on the Internet.

It was a fast and happy song. Marvel began stomping his hoof wildly to the rhythm of the song. He stomped so hard, he disappeared inside a cloud of dust!

Eva kept playing as long as she could, but the dust began to tickle her throat. She started coughing and laughing…coughing and laughing…Marvel laughed along, from deep in his belly.

"I love you, Marvel! I can't see you through all the dust in here, so I'm going to wish you goodnight. I'll see you tomorrow."

Eva bolted out the barn door with a smile on her face and Marvel kneeled down in the barn to stay comfortable until Eva returned.

~ 9 ~
SCHOOL'S CANCELLED!

That night, deep in sleep, Eva dreamed she was waiting for her mom in front of her school. A yucky, scary feeling filled her belly when she noticed there were no teachers around. *Where was Jip Jackal lurking? And where the heck was Mom?*

Eva felt irritated, remembering how many times she had told her mom she didn't feel safe hanging around the schoolyard where Jip could mess with her.

Still dreaming, Eva felt something furry touch her back. She jumped. "What the...?" She turned, and there was Marvel.

His big spotted head was gently stroking her back. She let out a long sigh of relief when she felt his caring touch.

Marvel's head felt warm, and his big, long black eyelashes tickled her neck. She was so comfortable, she didn't want to move. Marvel started nudging her, first softly and then more strongly. Eventually, the nudging became so intense that Eva was almost knocked out of bed.

Suddenly she heard, "Wake up, honey, you're dreaming."

Eva's eyes popped open from a deep sleep. It wasn't Marvel nudging her after all; it was her dad standing over her, gently rubbing her back.

Eva's dad was a tall, thin man, with short, brown hair and a mustache. He worked as a dentist for a local business called Dentists R Us. He always thought it was a silly name, but he enjoyed seeing people's teeth get white.

"Sorry to wake you, precious one. It's time for your mom and me to go to work. I know you'll be sad to hear this," he teased, "but school's been cancelled. An unexpected ice storm came through last night while we were snoozing, so we let you sleep in as long as we could. Your little brother Bo doesn't feel well, so maybe you can help take care of him, like a good sister."

As her dad was leaving the room, he said, "Have fun today and call us at work if you need anything."

Eva was excited that she would be able to hang out with Marvel for a whole day without her mom and dad around. She couldn't believe that there was actually a real live giraffe right here on her property and no one else knew her secret.

When she looked out the window, she couldn't believe her eyes. The ground and trees were covered with a thick, sparkly layer of ice that twinkled in the morning sun. Everything looked like crystal, and the trees seemed to be made of glass.

She threw on her scarf, skipped breakfast, and ran as fast as she could out the back door. The moment she reached the ice, she did a forward dive and slid on her belly all the way down the steep hill.

"YIPPEEEE!"

Flying off Bo's BMX ramp, she picked up so much speed she couldn't stop. She glided right through the front door of the old barn and smashed into some empty paint buckets at the end of her dad's workbench.

CRASH!

"Guess what, Marvel?" Eva jumped up and brushed herself off.

Marvel was startled. He whipped his head around, with a mouth full of ice-covered leaves that were stuck in his throat and mumbled, "May yeah mus ga fig la."

"That doesn't sound like Giraffe Language!" Eva said, laughing. "What on earth did you say?"

Marvel swallowed. "I wasn't expecting you."

"Well, guess what? Because of the ice storm, they cancelled school today. My mom and dad went to work and left me with my little eleven-year-old brother Bo, and he's sick in bed. I was hoping we could hang out and finish the third and fourth steps of the Giraffe Game."

"I'd be delighted," Marvel said with a swing of his tail.

"But before we get started, would you be willing to get me a blanket and some hot tea? I sure felt cold last night."

Eva ran off and returned as quickly as she could with a blanket from her room and some hot tea. "And I brought you a fresh bandage," she said, reaching for his leg and carefully pulling off the old one.

Once the new bandage was in place, she took the blanket and tossed it over Marvel's back. She'd never imagined that her pink and white polka-dotted blanket would ever have long giraffe legs coming out from under it!

Eva giggled, noticing how the polka dots and Marvel's giraffe spots looked funny together. Marvel twisted his long neck so that he could have a peek at his warm covering. He grinned and rolled his eyes, as Eva sat on the stool beside him.

"I have a question, Marvel. You'll probably think this is silly, but this morning as my dad was walking out the door, he said, 'Your brother's sick in bed, so maybe you can help take care of him, like a good sister.' It made me feel—I don't know—kind of weird.

"And last night, when I put my dishes in the sink, my mom called me a 'good girl.' I guess I'm supposed to feel good when I hear those kind of compliments, but instead I felt a little bit annoyed…like I was a dog in training or something."

Eva raised her voice. "Grown-ups make all these rules to follow, and if I play by their rules I get complimented, and if I don't, I get scolded."

Eva started talking faster and taking short, quick breaths.

"And I don't like it Marvel, because the older I get, the more new rules there are…and I'm really sick of all the rules, but there's nothing I can do about it...I wish grown-ups would stop sometimes and just leave me alone." Eva gasped, puffing out her cheeks.

Marvel's ears started to wiggle and he talked fast to keep up with Eva. "Sounds like you're feeling really, really frustrated and you'd like much, much, much, much, much more freedom to make your own choices."

"Yeah. I really am." Eva slowed down and let out a deep breath. "I would at least like to have some say about the rules, instead of having them forced on me." Eva sighed. "I really don't like it when my mom and dad praise me just to get me to do what they want me to do."

Marvel's neck straightened, and his ears perked up. He looked scared and whispered, "What was that?"

He heard the sound of faint footsteps approaching. Someone was coming. They'd be discovered. *Oh no!* Marvel looked scared and he froze, as if he wasn't sure whether to run or hide.

~ 10 ~
THE PLAN

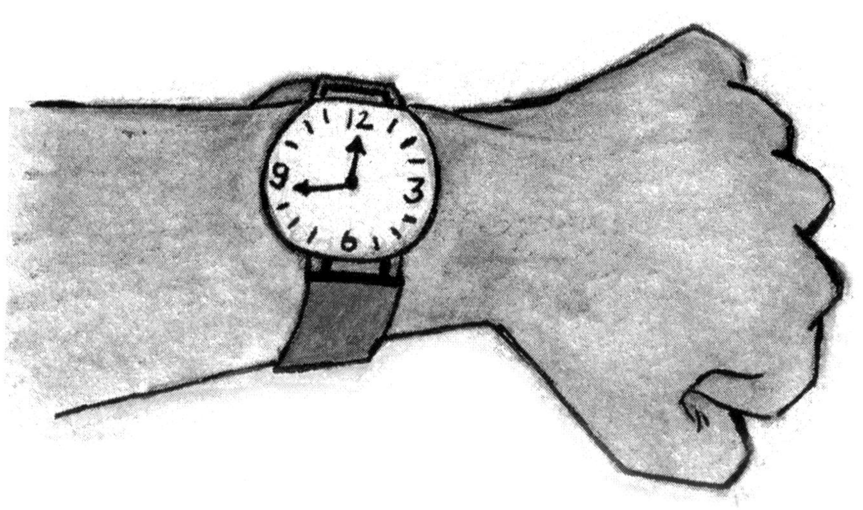

"Eva, are you back here?" a boy's voice called out. Marvel looked terrified, stuck his head under the old lampshade and got down on his knees.

"Oh, it's my best friend Ike. No need to panic, Marvel." Eva said reassuringly. Ike was twelve years old and pretty muscular for his age. He was shorter than Eva, but he made himself look a tad taller than her by dying his hair green and spiking it straight up in the air. His mom was half Hawaiian and his dad was part black and part Mexican, so it took a bright glowing green dye for it to be visible on his naturally dark hair.

"Hey Eva! I found you. Pretty cool that school's cancelled, huh?"

Ike said as he walked toward Eva. For the moment he was completely unaware of the company of an animal that was over ten times his size.

"Hey, Ike, this is Marvel."

Ike jumped back as soon as he saw the giraffe. His spiked green hair stood straight up on end, and he almost bolted for the door. "What the…?"

"Chill out, Ike. Marvel's cool. He's trying to find his mom and I'm helping him. Are you in?" Eva asked with a matter-of-fact look in her eyes—as if a misplaced giraffe was an everyday occurrence. She knew that Ike loved solving puzzles, and she was determined to get Ike's help.

Ike raised his voice. "Hold on a second, Eva. What are you doing with this giraffe, and how did it get here?" Ike put his hands on his hips. "I'm not going anywhere near that animal; it's about ten times my size, and I don't want it to get mad."

"Oh relax, Ike," Eva responded calmly. "This is Marvel. He's a talking giraffe, and he's all about helping people create peace in the world."

"Yeah, right," Ike muttered out of the side of his mouth. He began squinting his eyes and looking closer at Marvel. "What's with the lampshade…and the polka-dot blanket, Eva?" He started backing away. "You're playing dress-up with a wild animal? Have you gone mental?"

Marvel looked at Ike, and his ears began to wiggle. "Ike, are you freaked out about what's going on here?"

Ike's jaw dropped, and his eyes popped wide open. He shook his head violently back and forth. "No!"He looked at Eva. "I think I've fried my brain on TV and too many computer games."

"Ike, it's okay. This is Marvel the giraffe. He told me that kids are mostly the ones who can hear him speak—if, of course, they haven't forgotten how to listen. I'm learning his special Giraffe Language because I want to make friends with Jip Jackal…and I want to be able to talk to the adults who run the zoo so they'll really understand how much Marvel misses his mom. So are you in or what?"

"What!"

Eva pulled the blanket off of Marvel, and Marvel followed her lead by dropping the lampshade. "Look," she said, "he's just a normal giraffe."

"Yeah. Except that he talks and he's in your barn."

"Okay," Eva agreed, "that is sort of strange. But I promise, when you get to know him you'll love him. We made the friend pact."

Marvel lowered his head and parted his lips as much as he could, giving a big toothy smile. Ike's head tilted and he cracked a tiny smile.

"So," Eva asked, "do you want to help me find a way to get Marvel back to his mom? We don't have time to waste. Are you in or out?"

"Okay, okay," Ike said curiously, looking at the big giraffe smiling at him. "I'm sort of in. But I don't want to get in trouble. Something smells fishy about this, and I want to know how this giraffe got here. You know, it's probably illegal to have a giraffe in your barn."

Eva took a deep breath and let it out slowly. Everyone became silent. Eva and Marvel were staring at Ike. A fly buzzed and landed on Ike's hair. Nobody moved. Ike couldn't stand it anymore.

"Okay!" Ike swatted the fly from his hair. "So, you want to help him find his mom? Well, where is his mom?" Ike couldn't resist the challenge.

Eva smiled, knowing that, with Ike on board, things were going to get interesting. Marvel spoke up, looking relieved that Ike was willing to help. "All I know is that my mom was transferred to another zoo."

Ike rolled his eyes. "I still can't believe you're talking to me. This is too weird." Ike bent over, pulled his laptop out of his bag and started typing.

"Yes, I'm online! I can't believe I've got a connection down here. It's slow but it will do. Let me run a search." Marvel looked over Ike's shoulder curiously.

"All right!" Ike exclaimed after a few moments. "I found something. 'New Giraffe at the Riverbanks Zoo.' Is that her, Marvel?"

Marvel took a closer look at the picture on the screen. "That's her!"

"And by my calculations, the zoo is about sixty-five miles from here."

"So now what?" Eva's eyes widened.

Marvel responded, "Before we figure out a plan, I think it would help if you both knew what's most important to me right now. Would you like to hear it?"

They both nodded.

"Okay. Above all, I really want to know that my mom is safe and..."

Ike jumped in, "How about we put Christmas lights all over Marvel and take him to his mom's zoo?"

Eva interrupted, "And draw attention with all the blinking lights? No way!"

Ike thought hard, scrunching his lips, "We could put a blanket over him—a plain white one," he added, "not one with pink polka dots— and cut out eye holes."

Eva grinned. "That would only work if it was Halloween. A ten-foot ghost would scare people half to death! We're going to have to figure something else out."

Ike scratched his green hair and Marvel waited patiently. "I've got an idea. My Uncle Danny—you know, the one with the ice cream truck? He's the coolest. I'll bet I could get him to drive me over to the zoo in his ice cream truck. I could find your mom and check up on her. You could at least talk to her on my cell phone and see if she's okay."

"Hmmm, that probably won't work because my mom and I communicate mostly with our eyes. We also talk by mewing, bellowing, bleating, grunting, and snorting.

"Without eye contact, I won't be able to have a conversation with her that assures me that she's okay."

Eva, Marvel, and Ike bellowed, grunted, and snorted for another half hour and came up with a solid plan. They would drive Marvel to the zoo with his head sticking out of Uncle Danny's ice cream truck.

Ike would create an oversized giraffe mask to slip over Marvel's head. This would make Marvel actually look like a big make-believe giraffe used to attract business to the ice cream truck and no one would suspect that there was actually a real live giraffe under the mask.

They were all ready to set the plan in action. That night, Ike would call his uncle to set it up. Marvel reached out his hoof with the big grape-juice-colored wristband and placed it in Ike's hand. "This watch is pretty special to me, Ike, and as a way of saying thank you, I want you to have it."

Ike had never seen anything like it. He put it on and, though it was much too big for him, he proudly accepted. "Thanks. I think the Giraffe Language that you're teaching Eva is really cool. Maybe we could have an after-school club that helps kids learn. How about we call it the Giraffe Club? Or we could even start a website and name it www.GiraffeClub.org so kids everywhere could learn Giraffe if they wanted to."

Ike was onto something. "Man, if we could get Jip and his gang into this Giraffe stuff, maybe they'd chill out."

"Wow!" Marvel lifted his head. "Who would need to approve the after-school Giraffe Club to make it happen?"

Eva and Ike looked at each other glumly and both moaned at the same time, "Principal Pickle!" Their faces looked like deflated balloons.

"Are you guys feeling discouraged because you don't believe that Principal Pickle will support the project?" Marvel asked.

Ike responded, "I'm afraid of Principal Pickle. He tries to be nice, but he ends up acting more like a general who treats us like his soldiers."

"Are you worried that he won't care about what's most important to you?"

"Yeah. I think all he cares about is keeping order in the school. He doesn't care about the things that we kids care about like you do, Marvel."

Eva's stomach grumbled. She spoke up. "I'm hungry and I want to take a lunch break soon. What do you suggest that we do from here, Marvel?"

"How about writing a letter to Principal Pickle explaining why you want to create the Giraffe Club?"

Just then, Ike's cell phone rang. It was his mom wondering where he'd been. "Uh…well, Mom, I'm on my way home. I just got distracted, and Eva needed some help with something...Yeah, I'm coming now."

He hung up. "I'll get busy making the mask as soon as I get home." He winked at Marvel and Eva and darted off like a bolt of lightning.

Marvel and Eva sat in silence for a moment. Eva noticed a warm sense of relaxation come over her. Ike was on the project and his mind was set on helping Marvel.

She looked over at Marvel's big giraffe body and noticed the slow movement of his long eyelashes. As his eyelids lifted, their eyes met and time seemed to slow. In that unhurried moment, it felt as if the air between them wasn't space, but a connection—an invisible connection that she could practically feel in the air between them.

Eva looked more deeply into Marvel's eyes. It was as if they were both opening up, allowing the other to glimpse inside. For a moment, Eva couldn't tell who was who. It was weird. Even though Marvel was several feet away from her, it felt like they were touching—almost as if they were one person.

Time stood still. Eva imagined she could sense into Marvel's body and that she could feel his feelings. She became aware of a deep calm in him...a deep trust that everything was working out perfectly.

Eva slowly came out of this timeless connection when she noticed the unusual way the sunlight was colorfully moving on the walls. As the sun beamed through a huge icicle, it split the light into lots of little rainbows, which seemed to flutter by like butterflies.

Eva's eyes lit up. "Marvel! How about we go and check out the magical icicle wonderland out there? Everything looks like crystal. It's so cool. I've never seen anything like it.

"We can go out for just a couple of minutes. Mom and Dad won't

be home for a while and no one can see us from the street if we stay down here by the barn."

Marvel wiggled his long body and his tail. The blanket fell off his back and he bellowed, "I can't think of a better way to celebrate! Bring your guitar and harmonica!"

"Great! Let's do it!"

Marvel bent his head down as Eva tossed her purple scarf around his neck.

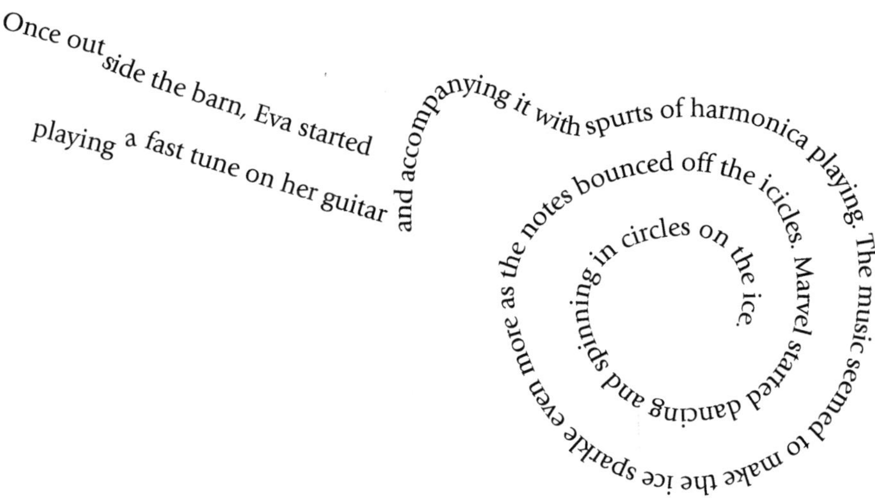

Sometimes Marvel's hooves would get stuck as they broke through the ice, adding a flurry of unintended dance steps. It took everything Eva had to keep playing her music instead of cracking up in laughter.

When Eva played her last note, they both flopped down on the ice. Eva was on her back with her arms outstretched. She watched the steam of her breath and marveled at the clear, crisp, blue sky.

Eva reached out to pet Marvel, enjoying the softness of his fur. She released a long slow breath…feeling relieved that she finally had a plan to help her new friend see his mom. Soon!

Eva headed back to the house to check on her brother, and to fix some lunch for everyone.

~ 11 ~
THE MYSTERY OF THE NEED

Eva fed her brother Bo lunch and waited till he fell back to sleep before she snuck out of the house with an entire bag of carrots and a big bucket of water for Marvel. As she arrived at the barn, it started to drizzle. Marvel and Eva listened to the sound of light raindrops hitting the tin roof.

Eva was still finding it hard to believe that there was actually a giraffe in her dad's workshop. The night before, she had checked out the Internet to learn a little more about giraffes.

She discovered a lot of interesting things—like they only need between ten minutes and two hours of sleep per day. How cool is that? More time for fun.

But, there were two facts that really stuck out to her. The first was the size of a giraffe's heart. Because giraffes need to pump the blood all the way up their long necks they have the largest hearts of any land mammal. This kind of explained why she felt such a warm, loving feeling when she hung out with Marvel.

The second thing she learned is that other grazing animals like to hang out with giraffes, because their height gives them an advantage for seeing predators such as lions coming. Other animals feel safe in the company of giraffes.

Eva noticed how safe she was feeling. "Marvel, that must be really cool to be able to see far into the distance with your long neck."

"I like to think that we giraffes not only can see far into the distance, but we also have a big view that enables us to see things that others don't always see.

"For example, we can see that, instead of always rushing to try to get our own way, it works out better sometimes if we take our time to understand and care about what others want too. Especially if we want them to care about us."

Eva sat down and pulled her knees to her chest. "Do you think we can finish the third and fourth steps now, Marvel? I really want things to change at school with Jip. I mean…I actually really do care about him. He used to be my best buddy when we were little, so I don't get why he started bullying me and the other kids at school when he got older."

"Well, as usual, you're right on cue, Eva. Answering that question is the third step. And it's one of the most important steps to the Giraffe Game. I call it 'uncovering the mystery of the need.'

"You see, there's a special way that giraffes try to answer the question, 'Why does Jip do what he does?' And it's different than the Blame Game. In the Blame Game, to answer the question 'Why does Jip do what he does?' is often answered with a judgment of what's wrong with Jip. Do you know what I mean by a judgment?"

Eva shrugged her shoulders, "Kind of…but not exactly."

"Here's an example of a judgmental thought: 'There are givers and takers in this world and Jip is a taker' or 'Jip is selfish', or how about this one Eva, 'Jip is a bully'.

"If I think these kind of judgmental thoughts, I'm playing the Blame Game because it immediately makes Jip wrong no matter what he does. It points the finger of blame at Jip...as if Jip was born with something wrong with him and he'll never be able to change."

Eva picked up some crayons and started drawing colorful circles as she listened along.

"What if Jip is having a challenging time getting along with his mom and dad and he doesn't know how to deal with it? And he's just acting out because he's never learned another way to make himself feel better?

"What if Jip was able to learn another way that didn't involve hurting other people? Or what if he learned to improve his connection with his mom and dad? Maybe that would change the way he's been acting in school."

Eva crossed her hands, "I understand what you're saying, Marvel, and it makes sense, but it's still not okay the way he treats me."

"I agree, Eva." Marvel looked at Eva and his ears began to wiggle. This time he didn't even have to say a word and Eva felt understood.

Marvel smiled and looked down at the ground to try to remember where he left off. "The point of all this, Eva, is if I judge Jip by thinking the thought, 'Jip is a bad person', I don't believe it will improve my connection with Jip. People can sometimes just tell if we're thinking these types of thoughts about them...and I don't feel optimistic it will support Jip in changing his ways.

"What I find to be more helpful...and a lot more fun for me too... is to play the Giraffe Game. Instead of judging Jip, my goal is to try to uncover the mystery of Jip's needs."

Eva moved closer to her giraffe friend. "What exactly do you mean by Jip's needs?"

"Hmmm..." Marvel seemed stumped for a moment on how to explain. He got into an awkward position, reaching his hoof to his chin.

"Isn't this what humans do when they're thinking hard about

something?" Marvel couldn't hold the position any longer and toppled over, sending the ladder to the ground with a thud. Eva and Marvel laughed out loud.

"So..." Marvel tried gathering his big body back up, but knocked a few rakes and shovels over on the way. Disregarding the slight commotion, he picked up where he had left off. "What is a need?

"Well, Eva, since people don't often talk directly about needs, they can be tricky to describe. I think the easiest way to explain needs is by playing a simple fill-in-the-blank game. I'll start a sentence, and you finish it by guessing the need. Ready?"

Eva's eyes twinkled. "Sure."

Eva picked up the ladder and put it back in its place.

"I'm feeling hungry because I have a need for...?"

GIRAFFES SAY:

step #3: NEEDS. Giraffes pay very close attention to the universal needs that all people share.

"Food."

"Okay, let's do a couple more. I'm feeling tired because I have a need for...?"

"Rest."

"Yup. I'm feeling thirsty because I have a need for...?"

"Water."

"Exactly. Those are basic needs that all people have, right? If these needs aren't met, it's hard for people to remain peaceful, because they need these things to survive.

"One of the keys to creating peace and harmony between people is to pay very close attention to their needs. And the kind of needs I'm talking about are ones that all people share...I call them universal needs. This means that everyone on the whole planet has them.

"Let's try a few more examples. Ready?

"I'm confused because I'm needing...?"

"To understand?"

"You've got it. Here's another one:

"I am feeling overwhelmed because I am needing...?"

"Umm...teachers to give me less homework?"

"Well, that's actually not a need that everyone shares. It's something specific that you would like your teachers to do. We call that a strategy, not a need. Strategies are specific. For example, food is a need and broccoli is a strategy. Everyone has a need for food but not everyone enjoys broccoli."

GIRAFFES SAY:

NEEDS instead of STRATEGIES:
Food is a need.
Broccoli is a strategy.
Everyone has a need for food, but not everyone enjoys broccoli.

The way Marvel's tail swished back and forth gave Eva the feeling that he was really excited. He started stomping his back hooves in a little celebration dance.

"Before we move on to step four, Eva," Marvel went on, "let's do one more quick guessing game. I'll give you an example, and you guess if it's a need or a strategy. Ready?"

"Ready!" Eva replied, getting on all fours and doing an imitation of Marvel scratching his chin.

"Here we go." Marvel gently pushed Eva and she tumbled over. "I need Jip to tell me more jokes.' Is that a need or a strategy?"

Eva smiled at Marvel. "That's easy. It's a strategy because not everyone on the planet wants Jip to tell them jokes."

"You got it. So what's the need, Eva?"

"Umm…Fun? And maybe even friendship? I think those are needs because pretty much everyone on the planet has a need for fun and friendship. Even grown-ups."

"Even us giraffes too!" Marvel wrapped his neck around Eva and lifted her up into the air.

"Hey!" Eva squealed with her feet dangling to the side. "I'm scared of heights. Put me down!"

Marvel brought Eva to the ground gently.

"Thanks, Marvel." Eva gave Marvel a big kiss on the side of his face. "Hey, are we done with step three? Can we go on to step four now?"

"You just did, Eva! It's all about making requests!"

~ 12 ~
RELISHING REQUESTS

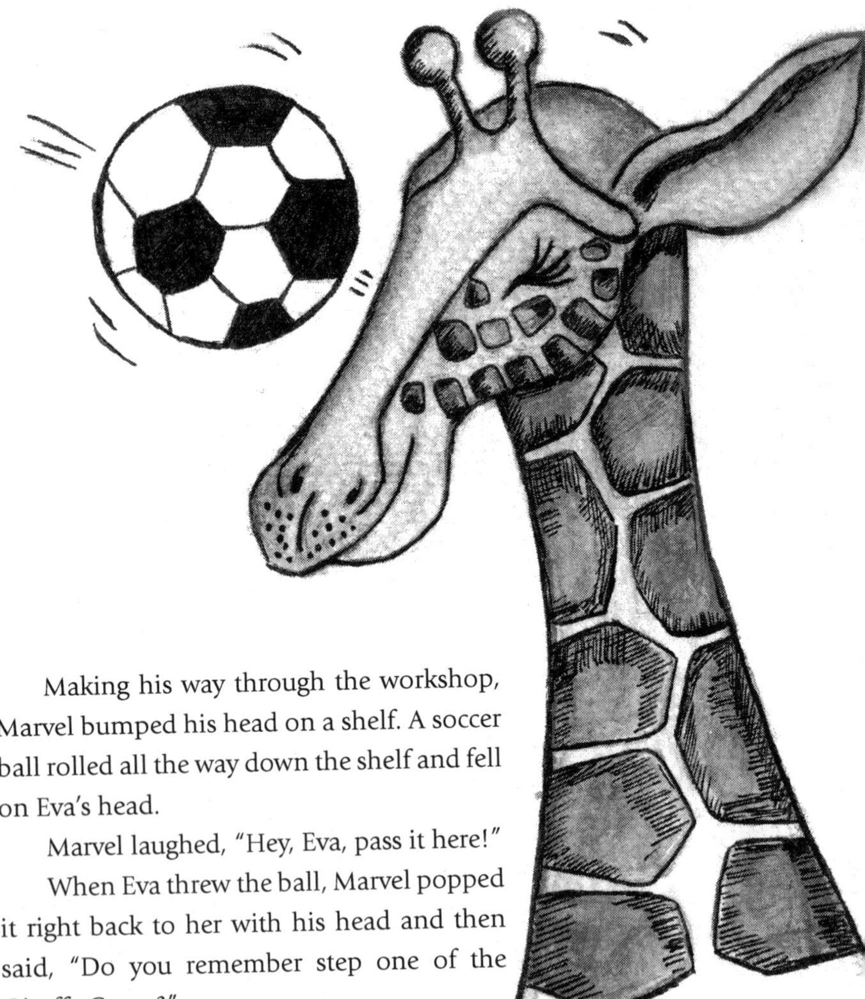

Making his way through the workshop, Marvel bumped his head on a shelf. A soccer ball rolled all the way down the shelf and fell on Eva's head.

Marvel laughed, "Hey, Eva, pass it here!"

When Eva threw the ball, Marvel popped it right back to her with his head and then said, "Do you remember step one of the Giraffe Game?"

Eva rolled her eyes and guessed, "Observation?"

"Yup. What about step two?"

Eva went into a trance as she dribbled the soccer ball from one knee to the other...down to her feet and then up to her knees again. After about ten seconds Marvel's voice finally registered in her head and she realized she had been asked a question. "Oh! Feelings!" she exclaimed. Eva kept juggling the soccer ball without dropping it.

"Right on! And step three?"

"Needs!"

"And the fourth and final step of Giraffe Language is all about making requests." Eva caught the ball and placed it on the ground and Marvel went on with his rambling rhetoric. "This is a key step in Giraffe Language, because it lets us know exactly what to do if we want to make life wonderful.

"When requests are not clear, it can create confusion. I'll give you an example: let's say Ike said to his mother, 'I'm hungry.' Can you see that this statement might be a request in disguise?

"I find that this is not the clearest way to make a request, because now Ike's mother might go on a wild goose chase of trying to guess what he wants by saying things like, 'Would you like a sandwich?' 'Do you want a drink?' 'Would you care for some grapes?' But if Ike's mother asks, 'What's your request?' he can ask her for exactly what he wants."

GIRAFFES SAY:

Step #4: REQUESTS. Giraffes ask for exactly what they want, instead of making statements that leave others to guess what they would like.

"You know, Marvel, I just realized that I make a lot of statements instead of requests. Just this morning, I said to my mom, 'I can't find my shoes,' instead of actually asking her if she'd help me find them."

Eva kicked the soccer ball to Marvel as he began speaking.

"Another thing people often do is to express a wish instead of a request."

"Oh, you mean like when Bo kept wandering around the yard last weekend saying 'I wish I could find my skateboard?' I didn't even think about helping him because he never asked, added Eva."

"Exactly, Eva." Marvel knew that Eva was ready, so he launched a swift kick of the soccer ball straight at her belly. Fast as lightning, Eva surprised him by punching it right back with her fist.

GIRAFFES SAY:

REQUESTS instead of WISHES: Giraffes make requests directly to others, instead of speaking wishes and secretly hoping that others will help them.

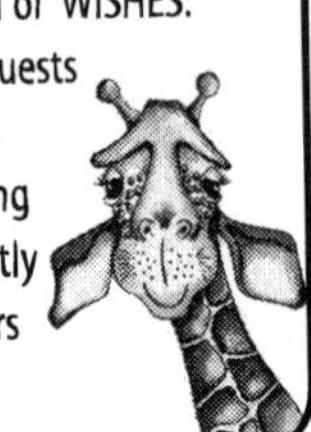

"WHOOP!"

Marvel hooted, ducking his long neck to avoid a smack in the nose. He chased the ball across the floor.

"And here's one more tip for you: it's important not to make backward requests." Marvel shot the soccer ball back to Eva and she caught it.

"What's a backward request?"

"It's telling someone what you don't want, instead of what you do want. Let's say Jip Jackal is pulling your hair and you say, 'Stop pulling my hair.' So he stops pulling your hair and starts poking you. So you say, 'Stop poking me.' Then he starts pushing you.

"Can you see how it doesn't work very well when you tell someone what you don't want? If you want to get your needs met, it helps to tell people exactly what you do want."

"I know what you mean, Marvel. The other day, my history teacher asked two girls to stop whispering, so they started passing notes behind his back instead. I guess when you tell people what you don't want, it doesn't always help you get what you do want."

GIRAFFES SAY:

Giraffes understand that asking for what they don't want doesn't always help them get what they do want.

"Exactly Eva. And there's one last thing I want to share with you about Giraffe Requests. Do you want to hear what it is?"

"Sure, Marvel. I'm with ya."

"The last thing to understand about Giraffe Requests is to make them as clear as possible, so others know exactly what you would like. So if I say, 'give it here,' you might not know what I'm talking about. But if I want to be clear I may say, 'Would you please pass the soccer ball to me now?'"

Eva passed the ball to Marvel, and he began rolling it around under his front hoof.

"Maybe if I made a clear request to my dad, he would stop bothering me about cleaning my room."

"How about I'll make believe I'm your dad. What request would you like to make of me?"

Crossing her legs, and with the sweetest voice she could muster, Eva asked, "Dad, will you please stop bothering me about cleaning my room?"

"Thanks for playing along, Eva. There are two ways you can make your request more exact. Do you know what they are?"

"Oops...oh yeah. When I said, 'stop bothering me,' I made a backward request, because I was telling my dad what I didn't want him to do." She paused, "Oh. And I think the second problem is that I didn't tell my dad exactly what I do want him to do. Can I try again?"

"Yup. And this time, Eva, see if you can make the request in a way that lets your dad know that you really care about his needs, too. One way to do this is to ask him, 'Would this work for you?'" Marvel kicked the ball back.

"Okay, I've got it, Marvel!" Eva picked up the ball and began tossing it from one hand to the other. "Dad, it's my room, and I want to be able to do whatever I want with it.

"At the same time, I know you want me to learn to keep it organized

> **GIRAFFES SAY:**
>
> Giraffes care about the needs of others, not just their own. Asking "would this work for you?" is one way we can let people know that we care about their needs, too.

and clean. What if I clean my room once a week on Saturdays, and you can come check to see if it meets your approval?"

Eva smiled, knowing she was on a roll. "Then," she continued, "the rest of the week I get to keep it however I want. Dad, will you tell me if that works for you?"

Eva tossed the ball back to Marvel, and he started bouncing it on his head in celebration. "Wahoo, Eva! You made a Giraffe Request that considers your dad's needs and also lets him know exactly what you would like him to do. I'm so stoked, Eva! We've actually completed all four steps of the Giraffe Game!"

They both cheered. Eva whipped out her harmonica and blew a long

"TAAAAA DAAAAAAHH!"

The two of them danced a little jig.

Marvel smiled at Eva. "Can I share with you what I loved so much about that request you just made?"

Eva nodded.

"When you asked your dad if your idea would work for him, you made it clear that you didn't have to have it only your way. I could tell you were willing to listen to him and find a way that would work for both of you."

"Yeah, Marvel…wow, that's so different from how I usually talk!"

"People don't usually like demands, Eva. They like to have a choice."

"I can relate. I sure wish you could teach this stuff to my mom. I don't like it when she bosses me around. It takes all the fun out of helping her, and to tell you the truth, it makes me want to do just the opposite."

"I know what you mean, Eva. That's why I only want others to help me if they are willing to do so freely. Have you ever seen a small child feeding a hungry duck?"

~ 13 ~
HUNGRY DUCKS

Marvel waddled around and tried to make the sound of a duck. "Snort. Snort." Eva smiled and put her hand over her eyes and shook her head to hide her embarrassment.

"It's funny, Marvel," Eva went on. "A few weeks ago, we took my four-year-old cousin Joey to the lake for his birthday, and he had so much fun feeding the ducks. It was like all

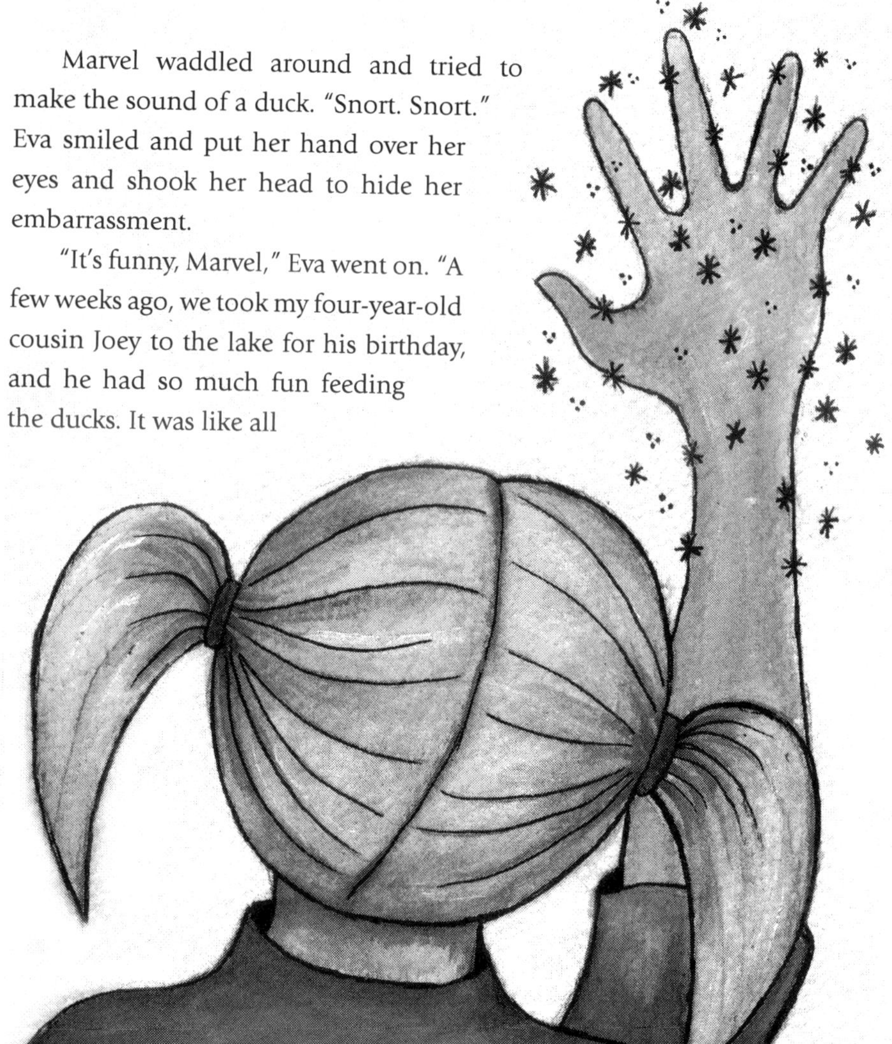

GIRAFFES SAY:

REQUESTS instead of DEMANDS: Giraffes make requests in a way that allows others to say "yes" freely and joyfully like a young child feeding a hungry duck.

the ducks came to join his party!"

"And I'll bet you could hardly tell who was getting the gift—Joey or the ducks."

Eva smiled. "That's right, Marvel. Joey didn't even want to open his birthday presents because he was having so much fun giving to the ducks."

Marvel scratched the ground with his front hoof as he spoke. "I believe that people naturally love to help others, and when we make requests instead of demands, we give them the opportunity to feel the same kind of joy Joey felt when he was feeding those ducks."

"Wow, Marvel. That's how I felt when I gave you the green tea with the cinnamon stick. It's kind of like your request was actually a gift to me. Like you gave me a chance to give back to you! I loved that!"

Eva spun around on one foot. "Hey, Marvel. How about we share some kiwi fruit to celebrate our finishing all four steps of the Giraffe Game? My mom bought a whole bag of them for me yesterday at the farmers' market. They're so yummy. How about I peel some and bring them for us to share after dinner?"

"You don't have to peel mine, Eva. I love them with their furry skin still on!"

Eva made a funny face. "Oh yeah, for a minute I forgot you were a giraffe!"

Her cheeks were glowing rosy red. When she looked in Marvel's eyes, she could see a reflection of her whole body. Eva felt a wonderful sense of connection with Marvel and everything around her. Her eyes began to well up with tears of joy.

Marvel became blurry. As the light passed through the tears in her eyelashes she saw rainbows. But the rainbows weren't outside, they were inside of her. She imagined that she could see every cell in Marvel's body twinkling like a million tiny stars.

Looking down at her hands, she saw the same tiny stars. It was as if each cell in her body had a life of its own. What was happening to her? Time stood still, and the whole world seemed to shimmer with beautiful colors.

She imagined she was waking up from a dream, but the dream was real...Eva was waking up to the magic of being alive...She cuddled her body up against Marvel's back leg and put her hand gently on his belly. They both remained silent as they drank in the sweetness of the moment.

After a while, Eva remembered Bo. "I'm going back to the house to check on my brother. I'll be back with those kiwi fruits in a little while."

"Bye, Eva."

"See you later, Marvel."

~ 14 ~
BECOMING ONE WITH THE WAVE

After dinner that night, Eva brought some leftovers for Marvel, and a bowl of sweet, green kiwi slices for herself— and four fuzzy brown fruits for Marvel. When she entered the barn, she saw him sitting on his knees with his head down.

"Are you all right, Marvel?" she asked, placing the food on her dad's workbench.

"At the moment I'm feeling sad and concerned, because I don't know if my mom's comfortable and happy at the new zoo."

Eva's ears wiggled as she listened in the same way she learned from Marvel. "Are you worried, Marvel, because you want to know that your mom is okay?"

Marvel breathed a big giraffe sigh. "Yeah. Thanks for being here for me, Eva. I was really needing some empathy."

"What is empathy, anyway, Marvel? I've heard the word, but I don't know what it means."

Marvel closed his eyes and raised his long neck, "Here's one way to explain: Have you ever seen someone surfing a wave who has lots of experience? They make it look really easy because they're so connected to the wave that they seem to become one with it."

Eva tilted her head in such a way that Marvel knew she wasn't quite getting it. "Here's an easier example. Have you ever read a book while having a headache and you got so involved in the story that you forgot your pain?"

"I know what you're talking about, Marvel. I love when that happens. I remember one time I was watching a movie and I had poison ivy so bad I couldn't stand it. But then I got so into the movie that I stopped itching. I totally forgot I had poison ivy."

"That's exactly what I'm talking about, Eva. Empathy is something that happens when you're so focused that you fully connect with the thing you're focused on. Have you ever had the experience of being upset and having a friend listen in a way that helped you feel a lot better?"

"That happened a couple months ago with my friend Tara. She slept over, and we stayed up all night whispering and telling stories... talking about boys, and making shadow puppets on the wall with a flashlight.

"We had so much fun together that we forgot how late it was until we heard the morning birds start singing. I like Tara. She even understood why I've been so bummed out about Jip Jackal."

"Empathy, Eva, can sometimes be that wonderful warm experience of sensing that someone else is deeply connecting with us and accepting us as we are.

"And if I want to help another person have that experience, I don't give them advice or try to fix their problems. Instead, I listen to them in a special way. I become curious and I sincerely care about what's most important to them in each moment…I listen for their feelings and needs.

GIRAFFES SAY:

GIRAFFE LISTENING, is the gift of bringing my curiosity to what's most important to another.

"I call that Giraffe Listening. It's the way I've been listening to you, Eva."

"Wow! That must be why I get the feeling that you always understand me. I love Giraffe Listening! And I like it a lot better than that thing that people sometimes do—you know, when they pretend that they're listening, but they're really not. They're just sort of waiting to say what they want to say next. Marvel, how do I get better at listening like a giraffe?"

Marvel looked to the left and then to the right, as if he was about to give away his deepest secret.

"One of the easiest ways to practice Giraffe Listening is to just be silent and listen. It's really a lot easier than talking, once you get the knack of it. And while you're silently listening, you can make believe you're a detective who is trying to uncover the mystery of the other person's feelings and needs.

"But because most people haven't learned to talk about their needs, it can be tricky. For me, that just makes it a really fun wave to ride! If I stay focused and listen carefully for what's most important to the other person, I stay on the wave. If I start thinking about what's wrong with the other person and play the Blame Game, I fall off."

GIRAFFES SAY:

One trick to GIRAFFE LISTENING is to just BE SILENT, while keeping your curiosity focused on the other person's feelings and needs.

"Well, what about when someone's mean to me, like Jip Jackal? What do I do then?"

Marvel responded, "That's some of the magic I've been telling you about, Eva. When I listen with giraffe ears on, I'm protected. I don't let others upset me, because I don't listen to their opinions and insults. No matter what they say, I just listen for the feelings and needs in their heart.

"Believe it or not, when I do this, I actually start to care about the other person, even when they're saying things I don't agree with. This can be tricky at first, but I'm sure you'll get plenty of practice with Jip Jackal around." Marvel smiled.

"Oh, Marvel—I lost track of time. It's 8:50 PM, and I told my mom I'd be getting ready for bed by nine. So how about this..." Eva smiled at the opportunity to try to make a Giraffe Request. "Marvel, would it work for you if..."

GIRAFFES SAY:

Giraffe Listening protects you from insults. With giraffe ears on, you stop hearing a person's negative opinions and instead, you start listening for what's in the other person's heart.

Marvel leaned toward her, and she couldn't resist wrapping her arms all the way around his long neck. She liked the way he smelled and the feeling of his fur against her face.

Eva began to lower her voice. "Well...I had hoped we could take our time with this celebration. I was going to ask you if you would tell me some stories about growing up with your mom in the zoo while we ate the kiwi fruit. But now there's not enough time to do both. Do you still want to eat some of these sweet furry guys now anyway?"

Marvel snorted in delight, the way giraffes do when they're happy.

Marvel announced, "Three seconds on the shot clock!" Then he turned his mouth to the ceiling and opened it wide, like a basketball net.

Eva tossed one of the fuzzy brown fruits high into the air and Marvel caught it. Holding it in his mouth without chewing, he made a wide-eyed face and pointed with his nose in the direction of Eva's fruit bowl. He waited for her to take her first bite, so they could enjoy their dessert together.

Eva spooned up one of the round, green, black-speckled jewels and popped it into her mouth.

"Yummmmmmmmm!"

they both exclaimed with big smiles.

"I haven't enjoyed kiwi fruit since I was a baby giraffe. Yum! Toss me another one, would you?"

The two friends gobbled down their glistening green goodies and then Eva looked at her watch. It was 8:56. Gently, she touched Marvel's face and whispered in his furry ear, "Ike told me that on the day after tomorrow his uncle will take you to see your mom. So have sweet dreams, Marvel. You'll be seeing her soon."

Eva pulled her harmonica out of her pocket and played a slow, sweet lullaby as she strolled out of the barn. She turned around, blew him a kiss and then sprinted up the hill to her house with a warm feeling in her belly.

~ 15 ~
PUTTING PLANS INTO PLACE

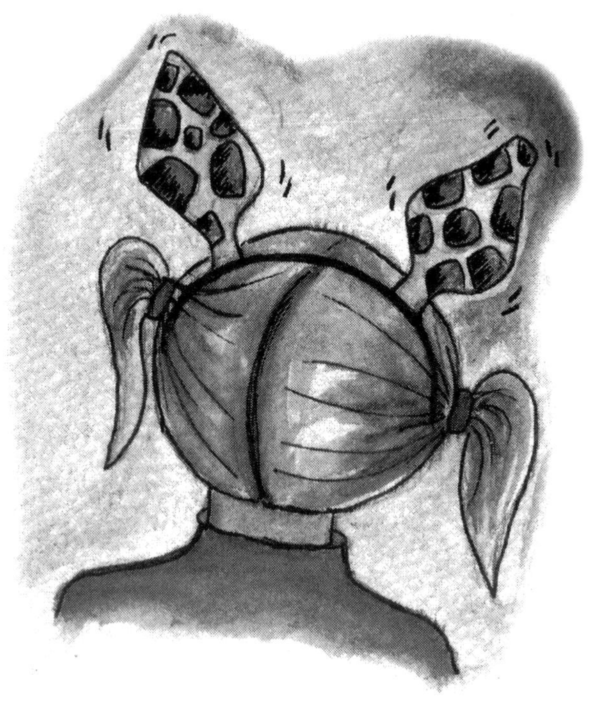

The sound of her alarm clock yanked Eva out of her warm, pleasant dreamland. It was a cold, rainy Wednesday morning, earlier than most people would want to greet the world, and Eva did not feel the least bit like getting out of bed.

Her eyes struggled to open, then drifted closed, then opened, then closed…until she finally reached the surface of her waking reality. Groggy and disoriented, dreading the exit from her warm bed into the cold morning air, Eva covered herself in her quilt, and dragged herself to the bathroom.

I wish I didn't have to go to school today, Eva thought to herself. *Hanging out with Marvel yesterday was so awesome.*

After grabbing a banana, she went out the side door through the garage. Her mom was waiting by the car in her workout clothes and her short blond hair was neatly combed with every hair in place.

Bo was already in the car. He was wearing a Michael Franti t-shirt that was a bit too short and it allowed his pudgy belly to be exposed. "I don't want to go to school today," Eva told her mom.

"Eva, there are some things in life we have to do whether we like them or not. You have to go to school and if you carry on about it, I'm not taking you to Tara's house this weekend.

"And furthermore," her mom was suddenly on a roll with her lecturing, "if your grades don't improve, your bike privileges will be taken away. I need to see you start taking responsibility for yourself!"

Feeling heavy-hearted, Eva got into the car. Bo was waiting inside with a smirk. He poked her. "Why are you so quiet?"

"Leave me alone!" She felt annoyed and wanted her brother to give her some space.

Bo had a hunch that Eva was hiding something.

"You're keeping a secret. You're acting funny," he teased.

"Leave me alone, Bo!"

Just then their mom barked, "If things don't settle down in here, you'll both be grounded!"

How could someone who smells like yummy Easter cookies talk like that? Overwhelmed, Eva couldn't remember anything she had learned from Marvel, so she decided to just keep her mouth shut.

When they arrived at school, Bo got in one last poke and then he blew his mom a kiss goodbye.

There was a talent show that day in the auditorium. Kids danced on the big blue stage and ran around in weird masks. Jip Jackal was secretly shooting spitballs through a straw at the backs of people's heads. Eva felt like busting him by telling a teacher what he was up to but she kept it to herself because she didn't feel much like talking.

She was kind of bummed because this year she decided not to join the talent show. Last year she came in first place by playing her bright blue guitar and her harmonica at the same time. But because of all the attention she got, Jip Jackal started bothering her even more. She decided it wasn't worth the trouble to go through that again this year.

As she was leaving school that day, Jip came up behind, pushed her, and squealed, "I'm thanking you on behalf of the whole school for not playing that wimpy blue guitar this year! My ears are still recovering."

Eva stood there gritting her teeth as she watched Jip run off with a football in one hand and his faded jean jacket in the other. She felt angry that, no matter what she did, Jip wouldn't leave her alone.

As she walked through the schoolyard she slouched her head down towards the ground, feeling a bit disappointed with herself. One of her favorite things was to see the smiles on people's faces when she played music.

She remembered how both teachers and students alike told her how much fun they had at the talent show last year, and she told herself that she would never again let Jip stand in the way of her playing music.

When Eva got home, she couldn't wait to talk to Marvel. She was surprised to find him dusting the shelves with his tail. "I'm just cleaning up a little after that dust storm we made when I was stomping along with your harmonica the other day. What's up, Eva?"

"Oh, I don't know," she said with slumped shoulders. "I'm just a little bummed because I had a hard day with Jip. The day kind of started out on the wrong foot when my mom started lecturing me on how I had to get to school. I forgot everything you taught me about the Giraffe Game. I wish my mom talked to me a little more like you sometimes."

Eva leaned up against Marvel and rubbed her cheek on his big round belly, feeling his soft fur against her skin. She took a few deep breaths and, as she relaxed into Marvel's silent empathy, a tiny spark of optimism returned.

With a hopeful high-pitched voice she asked, "Can we practice again the way we did yesterday? I want to hear what it would be like if

DICTIONARY
DICTIONARY

my mom talked like a giraffe."

"Okay, Eva. How about this? I'll make believe I'm your mother with giraffe ears on and you can speak any way you like."

Eva shared some of the things that her mom said earlier that day and Marvel jumped right into his role as Mom. "It's time to go to school, Eva. I'm feeling concerned about the time and I'd like to go now." Eva started to grin from cheek to cheek, hearing Marvel trying to make his voice sound chirpy like her mom.

But she took a breath and focused her attention back to her part in the role-play. She imagined herself standing in the driveway by her mom's car. She decided to act like she was in a bad mood.

"I don't want to go. I don't like all the boring stuff they teach me."

Marvel responded, still making believe he was Eva's mom, "Are you frustrated with what's being taught at school, honey?"

"Yes!" Eva exclaimed. "I'm never going to use the stuff they teach us anyway!"

"Sounds like you're feeling annoyed about studying things that you don't see any point in learning."

"That's right, Mom. And worse than that, they don't teach us the stuff that really matters, like how to get along with other kids. They can't even help me with my problems with Jip."

"Eva, are you feeling disappointed because you want to learn things that really matter to you?"

"Yeah! And I don't like the way adults force me to learn things I don't care about. And then they say something annoying like..." Eva spoke with a whiny mocking voice, "'You'll thank me when you get older Eva'. YUCK! I can't stand that when grown-ups say those kinds of things to me. Things like, 'You're just a kid, and you'll understand someday'."

Marvel's ears started to wiggle and he moved closer to her. "Eva. I'm not sure about this, but do you feel annoyed when grown-ups say those kind of things because..."

Eva jumped in, raising her voice. "It's so annoying, Marvel! Just because I'm younger doesn't mean I don't understand! And it doesn't mean I'm inferior! It really gets on my nerves when grown-ups act like they're superior."

Eva leaned up against the doorframe of the barn and hung her head toward the ground. After a while, she noticed Marvel was still standing there listening to her. She started to relax.

"I know that my mom and dad want to help me. And most of the time they do. But sometimes I wish they could listen to what I have to say before they make me do things I don't want to do.

"It's hard for me because, whenever I get angry, I really don't want to listen to a word they have to say and I know that only makes things worse. Could we do another practice round, Marvel, where I get to be the giraffe and I can practice listening?"

Eva took a sip of water and moved closer to Marvel.

"Okay, Eva. How about you be yourself with giraffe ears on and I'll be your mother as a…um…a jackal?"

Eva snorted **out a laugh** and the water **sprayed out her nose** and mouth, **almost hitting Marvel.**

Marvel couldn't hold back his laughter. "I see it's not only us giraffes that snort."

Holding her belly, Eva fell to the barn floor and giggled uncontrollably.

With a twinkle in his eye, Marvel said, "In honor of Jip Jackal, we can say that a jackal is someone that we sincerely want to connect with but we haven't yet learned how…someone we find hard to get along with."

Eva took several deep breaths to collect herself. "Cool. So you be my mom as a jackal and I'll be myself with…"

Eva reached for something hidden inside her jacket. "I'll be myself with giraffe ears on!" Eva swiftly pulled out a set of furry giraffe ears and put them on her head.

"Hey," Marvel marveled, "those look like my ears!"

"I found them in a wicker box where my mom keeps our old Halloween costumes. One year, my brother was a giraffe! I thought I might be able to hear like you if I had ears like you."

"Cool, Eva. This will help us keep track of who's the giraffe and who is the jackal. In this role-play, I'm going to be your mom as a jackal, right?"

"That's right, Marvel. And I'm going to be myself with giraffe ears on. Are you ready to start, Marvel?"

"Yup! Let's do it." Marvel raised his voice in that silly impression of Eva's mother. "It's time to go to school, Eva."

"Mom, I'm not feeling much like going to school today."

"There are some things in life you just have to do, whether you want to or not. You know you have to go to school."

"Mom, are you feeling concerned because you really care about my future?"

"That's right, Eva. Do we have to have the same arguments every day?"

"Mom, are you feeling annoyed because you want our mornings to be easier?"

"That's right. Thank you for listening. Now get in the car."

Eva reached up and touched the giraffe ears on her head, "Mom, since I want to make things easy for you right now, I'm ready to go to school. I'm also wondering if we could figure out a way that I can learn the things that I want to learn—things that they don't teach us at school."

"That sounds wonderful, Eva."

"Wow, Marvel. That went really well. I think I'm starting to get the knack of this Giraffe stuff," she said, doing a little dance, shuffling her feet in the dirt. "But," she stopped shuffling and looked up at Marvel, "I wish I could have done that with my brother Bo when he was bugging me today in the car. Can you be Bo as a giraffe?"

"Sure. I'll pretend that I'm Bo," Marvel said.

Eva showed her teeth and growled, "I'm going to be myself as a jackal," she said, pulling off the giraffe ears and tossing them aside.

After Eva fed Marvel some of the lines, he began pretending he was Bo. "You're awfully quiet today. Are you feeling okay?"

Eva played along, with a grouchy tone of voice. "I don't want to talk. You bug me."

"Are you feeling scared to talk?"

"You wouldn't understand."

"So you don't trust I'll understand what you're going through?"

"Yeah, you always tease me."

"I feel really bummed when I think about all the times I've teased you. In the future, will you let me know when I act in ways that you don't like, and I'll try to stop? I'm really trying to change my ways, Eva. I want us to get along, to be able to help each other."

Eva felt a lump in her throat. If only Bo were a giraffe.

"Oh…I forgot to tell you, Marvel, my buddy Ike and his uncle will be bringing the mask over, and you'll leave at around three o'clock in the ice cream truck. My mom and dad work late tomorrow, and Bo will be at baseball practice, so you can make a clean getaway without anyone noticing a thing."

Marvel was eager to finally see his mom again. "I'm so grateful for your friendship and support, Eva. I'm excited to tell my mom all about you—especially the way you jam on that harmonica! Where did you learn how to play like that?"

"I found a bunch of free lessons on the Internet. It was easy. I carry my harmonica in my pocket everywhere I go, so I can play any time I want. When I meet your mom, I'll definitely jam for her!" Eva flipped her harmonica from one hand to the other.

"I'll see you after school tomorrow, Marvel. Okay?"

"Great, Eva! I can't wait."

As Eva headed home for the evening, she felt joyful that she had finally found a way to help Marvel reconnect with his mom.

~ 16 ~
MARVEL'S MISSING!

The next day at school seemed to pass slower than a slug. Eva couldn't wait to get home to iron out the ice cream truck plan and return Marvel to his mom.

She ran inside, dropped her backpack on the couch and raced to the backyard. But when she approached the barn, she got a sinking feeling in her belly. It seemed too quiet.

She called out Marvel's name. There was no response, only silence. She checked around back and inside the barn. All she saw was the giraffe ears she had left there the day before. She picked them up and put them inside her jacket. *Where could he have gone?*

She trudged up the hill and back to the house to call Ike. Eva was so upset and confused that she almost stepped on her cat, Pumpkin. After three long rings, Ike picked up.

"Marvel's not here!" she whispered urgently. Just then, she heard someone coming toward the kitchen. "I've got to call you back!"

Eva's dad was home early from work, still wearing his white lab coat. Dr. Cassidy greeted his daughter. "Hi, sweetie."

"You...you scared me! I didn't know you were home," Eva choked on her words.

"I'm just here picking up some papers and then I'm going back to work."

"Oh." Eva nodded and made her way to the couch in the living room. She plopped down, found the remote control hiding under a pillow and started channel surfing.

Dr. Cassidy's voice came through from the other room. "Don't you have homework to do, young lady?" She felt uneasy when she heard the tone of her dad's voice.

"I'll do it soon." She shrugged her shoulders.

"Please get it done before you sit down to watch TV."

"Fine!" Eva threw down the remote, stomped up the stairs and slammed the bedroom door. She sprawled out on the floor, feeling irritated and angry, because she wanted more freedom to decide when she did things. She wished her dad were more like Marvel.

Her dad knocked sharply on the door. "Eva, I understand that you're upset, but I won't have slamming doors in my house. Is that understood? I expect you to get your homework done before watching TV. Where's your backpack?"

"Downstairs on the couch," Eva mumbled.

"Will you please go downstairs and get it, so that you can start your homework?"

"Yeah." She got up off the floor and stomped downstairs, feeling like she'd never be able to communicate differently with her dad. She had forgotten to use Giraffe Language again.

She grabbed her backpack and headed upstairs for the second time. With Marvel missing, she felt upset and was having a hard time concentrating on her homework. She didn't know if she'd ever see him again and the big lump in her throat became unbearable as she welled up with tears.

She went over and picked up her guitar. Usually just feeling the weight of it in her hands was enough to change her mood, but not this time. She was so upset, the only thing she could think of doing was to call Ike.

She secretly picked up the phone and started whispering, "Ike! It's an emergency! He's gone! Will you sneak through the side gate and look for clues? My dad said I have to stay in and study. Let me know if you find anything. I've got to go, Ike. Bye."

What could have happened to Marvel? Eva thought to herself. *I hope he's okay.* Eva felt an uncomfortable knot in her stomach. She thought about playing her harmonica, but even that probably wouldn't cheer her up.

Overwhelmed, she dropped down onto her bed to relax.

She slipped into an unexpected, deep sleep and had a really weird dream.

Her dad had big furry yellow giraffe ears that popped up out of his head and wiggled when he spoke.

"You seem to be really enjoying that show," he said. He sat next to her on the couch to watch TV and talk with her.

Eva started laughing. "Yeah, it's great," she replied, smiling.

When her dad spoke, it was from his heart. "I don't want to interrupt you, sweetie, but I'm feeling worried. I see the time and notice that you haven't done your homework."

"I'll do it later."

"I remember you told me that last night, and it didn't get done, so I'm concerned. Can you tell me what is keeping you from doing it?" he asked warmly. His neck began to grow into a giraffe's neck as his face stretched and distorted.

Eva moved a little further from him, "Well, I have a test tomorrow, and I don't like science," Eva explained. "The other kids get it so much faster."

In the dream, Eva's dad's ears started wiggling. "I guess it's not fun learning when you're not catching on as fast as the others. Are you worried that you will be teased for doing your work too slowly?" Eva saw something moving inside the backside of her dad's pants.

Eva replied cautiously, "Umm…yeah, I guess I'm a slow learner. I just don't like school sometimes."

"I'm really sad that you're feeling this way," Eva's dad said calmly. "I imagine that when you know how I care about your grades, it may be putting even more pressure on you. Are you worried about disappointing me?"

"Yes."

Dad's pants made a loud ripping sound. Eva jumped back to see a long yellow giraffe tail, with her dad's boxer shorts dangling at the end.

Eva's dad went on as if this was totally normal, "Well, first of all, honey, I don't believe you're a slow learner. I mean, maybe you don't learn some things as quickly as some of the other kids in your class, but I feel confident you can learn anything you put your mind to.

"If you want, we can go over your work together and I'll take the time to help you. Will you give me a chance?" Dad paused. "I don't want you to think you have to make me happy. I know you really care about your grades."

Just then Eva's dad exploded and black and yellow giraffe spots flew all over the TV room.

Eva woke up wide-eyed, gasping for air and totally freaked out.

When she realized it had been a dream, she began to calm down and laugh inside. *That was actually pretty cool,* she thought. *And even though it was one of the strangest dreams I've ever had, hearing Dad speak Giraffe was amazing!*

When she thought back to the fight they'd had in real life, she started wondering what her dad's needs might have been when he asked her to stop watching TV and do her homework.

I wonder if it's just that he really cares about me. Maybe he wants me to get good grades so that I'll have an easier time going to whatever college I want...and maybe he thinks this will give me more choices about making money in a way that's fun for me.

She felt compassion for her dad's needs, and at the same time, she was very aware that she wanted some freedom to make her own choices.

Wow. It felt amazing to pay attention to both her needs and her dad's needs. She wasn't making her dad wrong, and best of all, she started to believe that she could really learn to get along with her dad.

~ 17 ~
I SPY...?

Ike was determined to find out what happened to Marvel. He tiptoed through the side gate, hiding in the bushes along the fence line of Eva's backyard.

So that no one would see him, Ike cut a big branch with his Swiss army knife and stuck it down the back of his shirt with the leaves hanging over his head and shoulders. He used his mini-binoculars to search the yard and the area around the barn for clues to Marvel's disappearance.

After twenty minutes had passed, he still hadn't found a single clue. About ready to give up, he noticed an oddly textured patch of ground. Upon closer inspection, Ike realized that it was a clump of

Marvel's hair tangled around a leather string. It looked like he'd put up a fight. Ike pocketed the string. He would show it to Eva later.

As Ike stepped out of the old barn, Eva's brother Bo skidded up on his BMX bike. "Hey, what's up, Ike? Where's Eva?"

Ike was taken by surprise and shot up like a pogo stick, then stuttered, trying to figure out what to say. "She's studying. I'm...I'm... uh...looking for my watch."

"It's right there on your wrist," Bo interjected.

"Yeah...I found it." Ike put his hands in his pockets.

Bo popped a wheelie and screeched, "Great! Well, I'm heading inside for dinner."

"See ya," Ike waved. Close call.

"Wait, Bo! Can you ask Eva to come out here for a second?"

Bo went inside to get her. Eva came outside, biting her lip with a concerned look on her face.

"I found this." Ike showed her the evidence. "It's a leather string with Marvel's hair in it, and there are signs of a struggle." Eva looked awfully worried.

Her mom called out, "Dinner's ready, Eva! Come on in!"

"Coming, Mom!" Turning to Ike, she whispered, "We've got to figure out what happened to Marvel."

"We will," Ike reassured her. They parted ways and agreed to talk tomorrow.

~ 18 ~
INVESTIGATING IKE

After dinner, Ike looked out his bedroom window and spotted a police car parked in front of his house.

"Oh dang! The cops!" Ike ducked.

There was a knock at the door. Detective Beasley, a large man with a mustache, showed his badge. Ike's father let him in. With his ear pressed up against his bedroom wall, Ike spied on them.

"It seems that a giraffe was stolen from the local zoo, and a witness led us to believe your son may have something to do with it."

His dad defended him. "Our son Ike? What? Ike has always been very kind to animals."

"Well, if you'd let me speak to the young man," the detective said in a polite yet firm voice, "we could get this all straightened out."

"Well sure, you can talk to him. Ike!" his dad called out. "Would you please come here for a minute?"

Ike came out, trying to look like an angel.

"Son, I'm Detective Beasley. We have reason to believe you may be involved in a crime."

"Me?" Ike asked, as innocently as he could muster.

"Yes, you. Do you know the whereabouts of a giraffe stolen from the local zoo?"

"Um, no. I don't know where the giraffe is."

"Are you saying you have no involvement whatsoever in the giraffe's disappearance?"

"I have no idea where...uh...the giraffe is." Ike backed up a bit.

"Well, let me show you all a picture I have here of Marvel. That's the name of the missing person...um, I mean giraffe." Detective Beasley pulled the snapshot out of his shirt pocket. Marvel was smiling in the picture, and his grape-juice-colored watch stood out.

Just then, Ike's mom noticed the watch and blurted, "Ike! Doesn't that watch look just like the one in your room that you found the other day?"

Ike froze. "Does it?" He squinted and held the photograph closer to his face.

"You mean you've seen the watch of the missing giraffe?"

Ike stumbled over his words, "Um, well, sir, you see...I...found a watch that looks like that."

"You found a watch that looks like this one? Well, could you find the watch right now and show it to me?"

Ike hesitated and then walked to his dresser, sweating and holding his breath. He brought back Marvel's watch.

"Well, this does not look good. This is definitely the watch in the photo. We'll run tests just to be sure."

"Just because he found a watch doesn't mean he stole a giraffe!" Ike's mom said protectively.

The detective told them he was just doing his job, but because Marvel had been missing for more than twenty-four hours, an investigation was underway.

Ike was scared and couldn't believe this was all getting blamed on him. Many thoughts were racing through his head at once. Who the heck could have taken Marvel?

Detective Beasley told Ike's parents that they would be notified soon of the lab results. He walked out, writing in his note pad.

Ike's parents didn't believe their son was capable of committing a crime like that. It took a serious effort, and he answered a lot of questions, but Ike finally assured them that he didn't take the giraffe. His parents believed that he was telling the truth, but they sensed he was hiding something.

Later that night, Ike called Eva to share the news about Marvel. "Now what do we do?" he asked.

~ 19 ~
WIGGLING WILDLY

Eva was in her room. She was pacing and her mind was racing like a pet gerbil on an exercise wheel. *Who could have taken Marvel?*

Her mom peeked into the room and scrunched her forehead in frustration to see Eva still awake. "I thought you'd gone to bed already."

"I'm not tired," she told her mom.

Her mom raised her voice. "I'D LIKE YOU TO GET TO BED, NOW."

"I'm just not tired, Mom!"

Her mom's forehead appeared to split open and from inside came the voice of some prehistoric flesh-eating lizard, "IF YOU **DON'T** HAVE THE **LIGHTS OUT** IN **FIVE** MINUTES, I'M

NOT TAKING YOU TO THE ZOO THIS SATURDAY."

Eva swallowed. Oh no! Mom's in "LIZARD MODE." Eva knew that this was a perfect time to try Giraffe Language, but she felt so exasperated that part of her just didn't want to do it. She felt especially angry because she didn't like it when her mom forcefully took control and threatened to take away something Eva loved…just to get her way. Not only that, but Eva was also sick and tired of her mom telling her when to go to bed.

All of these thoughts were spinning fast in Eva's head and she was right on the edge of shouting back at her mom, but she knew this would only make matters worse. She decided to control herself and try to remember the things that Marvel had shared with her.

She closed her eyes, looked inside, and started to feel her feelings. Her chest was so tense it seemed her heart was tied in a knot. Eva suddenly became incredibly dizzy. She had been holding her breath longer than she realized.

Eva decided to slow down and start over. She began to relax and just feel her breath. She noticed her belly move in and out with each inhale and each exhale. She even sensed the rapid beating of her own heart.

Eva was amazed at how quickly she was able to relax by breathing deeply into the uncomfortable tension in her chest.

She then became aware of something she had never noticed before. The actual center of her body seemed to be underneath her belly button, deep inside of her. When she put her attention on this place in her body she felt strong and balanced. Her strength poured down her legs and when it reached her feet she imagined it grounded her like the roots of a tree.

When she opened her eyes, she was amazed to find that she was able to look outside and inside of herself at the same time. She saw her mom standing there in front of her, but this didn't distract her from steadily watching her breath move in and out.

Eva felt calm now. From this place of deep self-connection she began to sincerely care about her mom, especially because she knew the stress wasn't very good for her mom's health when she became the "LIZARD WOMAN."

Eva remembered that Marvel had suggested she try to sense the feelings and needs of the other person. At this moment, Eva had no idea what was going on for her mom. She also recalled Marvel saying that if she wasn't sure, she could just guess. *Well, I've got nothing to lose,* Eva thought to herself as she blurted out:

"Mom, are you annoyed because—?"

"Yes," her mom cut in. "I'm aggravated because it's your bedtime and I don't want you to get sick."

Eva's ears started to wiggle and – YES! – this time she actually started to sense her mom's needs: "Sounds like you really care about my health, Mom."

"That's right!" Mrs. Cassidy paused for a moment a bit stunned that Eva was actually listening.

They both stood there looking at each other and then Eva noticed the tension in her mom's forehead begin to relax.

"Is there something that you'd like to request of me, Mom?"

Eva's mom spoke more softly this time, "Well…as I said before… I'd really like for you to go to bed within the next five minutes so you don't get sick."

Eva's ears continued to wiggle, "Mom, I know that you really want me to take care of myself. At the same time, I'm nervous that I'm not totally ready for my test tomorrow. How about I stay up another half hour to study and then I'll go to bed?"

"Half an hour and no longer. Agreed?"

"Agreed." Eva's ears wiggled wildly. She had never seen her mom switch so quickly from "LIZARD MODE" to wanting to work together. *This Giraffe stuff is sweet!*

~ 20 ~
MARVEL'S MAZE

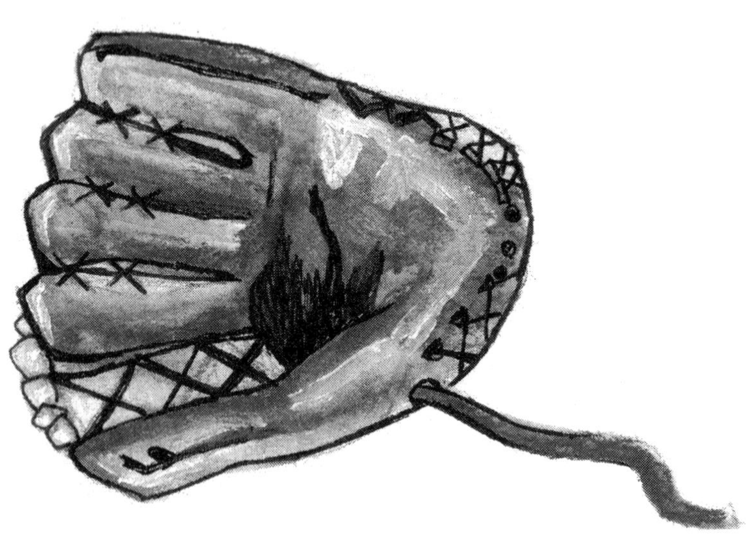

The next day, Bo stormed into the bathroom while Eva was brushing her hair. He was about to poke her when she noticed he was wearing a baseball glove. There was a leather string hanging from the glove and a hole where one was missing. Eva covered her mouth.

It couldn't have been. Why would Bo have anything to do with Marvel's disappearance?

"Get in here!" She pulled Bo by his gloved hand into the bathroom and shut the door quickly.

"What...?" Bo could barely get a word out before she confronted him.

"Okay, where's the giraffe?"

He turned a shade of red, then purple, actually just about the color of Marvel's grape-juice-colored watchband. It was obvious that he knew something. "I don't know what you're talking about."

Eva stared into Bo's eyes. "We know that whoever was involved in his disappearance left a leather string with his fur on it."

"What are you talking about?"

"The giraffe!" she said in a hushed scream, "WHERE IS HE?"

Bo looked down and quickly tucked his gloved hand behind his back.

Eva was so angry she totally forgot how to use Giraffe Language.

"Leave me alone, Eva! I don't know where Marvel is!"

"I KNEW IT. YOU'RE BUSTED! I never told you the giraffe's name was Marvel. SO START TALKING!"

Bo started to sweat. He locked the bathroom door.

"Remember that night when I slept over at my friend Zach's house last week?" Bo picked at his glove. "Well, Zach told me that he had a way of sneaking into the zoo from his backyard, and I thought it'd be fun. So we squeezed through a hole in the fence.

"It was a really dark night, so Zach used his cell phone to light our way. When we got to the giraffe's cage, we heard the zookeeper shout at us. We were about to get into a heap of trouble, so we took off like racehorses, but when I got back to Zach's house, I realized that my baseball cap must have fallen off when we were escaping through the hole in the fence.

"I started to panic, because Grandpa put my name in that cap, and I didn't want the zookeeper to find it and bust me. So I waited a couple of hours and then snuck back in to get it after Zach went to sleep. I was really scared.

"Just as I grabbed my cap, I heard a voice from up in the trees that said, 'Hello, my name is Marvel.' I couldn't believe my ears—a talking giraffe roaming free in the zoo! He told me that when the zookeeper ran after us, his cage had been left unlocked.

"After hearing that he was looking for his mom, I agreed to help him. I had to think fast. I remembered that Zach's mom had one of those small exercise trampolines in her backyard. I tore back to Zach's, got it, and threw the thing over the fence. I set up the trampoline and told Marvel the plan.

"At first he hesitated, but when we thought we heard the zookeeper coming, he took a running dash, jumped and bounced high over the fence. When Marvel hit the ground, all four legs splatted out beneath him. It was crazy, but he was okay!

"I couldn't keep him at Zach's, so I brought him to Dad's barn in the middle of the night. I knew you were taking care of him when I saw you bringing leftovers down to the barn and I just stayed away because I didn't want to get in trouble.

"When I heard on the news that the detectives were investigating, I freaked out and returned Marvel to the zoo so no one would find out."

Eva was on the verge of telling Bo what a fool he was, but then something came over her. Her ears wiggled. She remembered that Marvel had said to try to uncover the mystery of Bo's feelings and needs.

"Are you wanting me to understand that you were feeling scared about getting in trouble and you weren't sure what to do?"

"Yeah." Bo looked like the weight of the world had been lifted from his shoulders.

Then she told Bo that Ike was falsely accused of being involved in Marvel's disappearance.

"I don't want Ike to have to pay for this," Bo responded.

Just then, they heard, "Kids!" It was their mom. "What are you two doing up there for so long, flossing your toes?"

Bo opened the bathroom door and shouted downstairs, "Coming, Mom!"

Eva was nervous that Bo was going to get into big trouble and really sad that she no longer had a plan to help Marvel. It was amazing that Marvel's maze led back to Bo.

~ 21 ~
MARVEL MATTERS

Eva, Bo and Ike held a meeting in Dad's barn. When Ike found out that it was Bo who had taken Marvel back to the zoo, he was angry. How could Bo mess up their perfectly organized ice cream truck plan! He felt annoyed that he had worked so hard to make the big giraffe mask all for nothing.

Eva began the meeting. "First, I want to talk to the people who run the zoo, because I still want to figure out a way to get Marvel and his mom back together.

"Second, we need to prove that Ike wasn't responsible for taking Marvel. And third, I want to explain to the zoo board members that Bo's intention was to help Marvel and not to hurt the people who run the zoo.

"I think the best chance we'll have to help Marvel is talking with the zoo people. Since we're kids, I'm afraid they might not take us seriously enough to have a meeting with us. I wonder if we can make a deal with them.

"We can tell them that the person who really took Marvel is willing to confess if they are willing to meet with us for thirty minutes. I'll use Giraffe Language to help the board members understand why Bo took Marvel."

Bo was looking at the ground and holding his head in his hands.

Eva looked at Ike and her ears wiggled slowly, "Bo, are you feeling afraid that the people at the zoo won't understand your reasons for taking Marvel?"

Bo looked relieved that Eva understood. "I do feel scared, but I like the plan. I want to help Marvel and I don't want Ike to get in trouble for what I did."

Eva told them how Marvel had made it clear that he didn't want anyone to get in any trouble.

"He taught me his Giraffe Language. It's cool. I'll share it with you if you want. I have a good feeling that it's going to help us out a lot in this situation. I'm on your side, Bo. I'm going to do my best to help you."

Ike came up with the idea for them to make signs that read **MARVEL MATTERS!** They would stand up for the animals, to let everyone know that the animals' needs matter too.

That night, Eva had sweet dreams. Scented wild flowers flowed through the rolling green savannahs and giraffes roamed free.

When she woke up the next morning, Eva checked her computer and opened the e-mail she was looking for. The zoo board members were willing to meet on Saturday. Her plan was unfolding. So far, so good.

~ 22 ~
GIRAFFE JUICE

The next few days seemed to pass slowly. Eva missed Marvel and all the fun they'd had in Dad's barn. When Saturday finally arrived, she felt nervous about talking to the people who ran the zoo.

This was a real-life opportunity to try on her new giraffe ears, but she wasn't sure if she was ready. At the same time, she wanted to do everything possible to help Marvel reunite with his mom.

Eva's mom gave Ike, Bo and Eva a ride to the zoo half an hour before the meeting. That way, Eva would have time to talk to Marvel.

When she dropped them off at the entrance, they could smell popcorn in the cool spring air.

"Here's some money for your admission and some lunch. Now you kids take care of each other and call me if you want to come home early. Otherwise, I'll meet you back here at three."

As soon as her mom's electric-powered, boxy brown car was out of sight, Eva and the boys hurried to the ticket booth. Once inside, they immediately sped toward the south gate, where the giraffes and zebras lived.

"I can't wait to see Marvel!" Eva said excitedly. "Is it okay with you guys if I meet with him alone? I've got some major planning to do."

The boys nodded.

"Come back and get me ten minutes before our meeting."

Ike and Bo ran off to get some popcorn while Eva looked around, trying to locate Marvel.

Out of the corner of her eye, Eva saw something that made her heart sink. It was Jip Jackal feeding the goats in the petting zoo. *Oh no! What's he doing here?* She pretended not to see him and told herself that no matter what, she wasn't going to let him distract her from helping Marvel today.

When Eva saw Marvel, she got a bit choked up. The small cage he lived in upset her, but the warmth of his smile felt calming. She was relieved that no other kids were visiting the giraffes at the moment.

"Oh, Marvel, I'm so glad to see you! How are you? Are you comfortable? I don't like seeing you in that cage."

"Oh I'm fine for now Eva. The zookeepers treat me with care and feed me regularly. I just miss my mom. What's up with you Eva? You look a little stressed."

"Well, I just saw Jip Jackal here at the zoo and I'm feeling a little annoyed that, of all the days he could have chosen to come to the zoo, it had to be today..."

Knowing that Jip Jackal was lurking reminded her of how desperately she wanted to start the after-school Giraffe Club as soon as possible.

Oh, by the way," she went on, half out of breath, "I made an appointment with Principal Pickle on Tuesday afternoon to meet about the Giraffe Club. But I'm afraid that he won't want to hear a word I say. Do you have any ideas?"

"What is it exactly that you want to get out of the meeting?" Marvel asked thoughtfully.

"I want Principal Pickle to approve the Giraffe Club! That's all I care about."

Marvel snorted, "I'm concerned that if you go into the meeting trying only to get your way, and not caring equally about Principal Pickle's needs, he may not approve the project...even if he actually likes it."

"Well then how do I make him believe that I care about his needs?"

"It really doesn't matter how you do it. What matters most is that you really do care about his needs."

Marvel lowered his voice to a whisper, "What I'm about to tell you may really help."

GIRAFFES SAY:

EVERYONE'S NEEDS MATTER. Giraffes realize that if we don't care about other people's needs, they may not care about ours. Giraffes like to get their way, but only if it works for other people, too.

Eva closed her eyes, ready to drink in his words.

"Approach Principal Pickle with an open heart. Rather than trying to get your own way, listen for *his* needs. If he senses that you really care about his needs, he might start caring about yours. Then whole new solutions can become possible."

Eva put her hand on her forehead. "The truth is that, right now, I don't care about Principal Pickle. I don't think he'll take me or the club seriously."

"Are you feeling hopeless that he won't care about what matters to you?"

"Yeah. Grown-ups only care about grown-up stuff. I don't think he really cares about my needs. So how am I supposed to care about him?"

"Listen deeper. See if you can find ways that he is the same as you. Beneath everything Principal Pickle thinks, feels, or does, he is motivated by the same things you care about. Just like you, he has needs for fun, celebration and the love of friends and family.

"I know you may not like all the things Principal Pickle does, but if you turn your attention to the part of him that is the same as you, it will be easier to find space in your heart to care about his needs."

Eva nodded. "I've thought about this, but I've never heard it put in quite those words."

Marvel continued, "I believe that deep inside every person is a natural spirit that wants to take care of life: the life inside of other people and the life in all living things. This caring could be as simple as helping to cook a meal, planting trees, or recycling. Or it could be as big as protecting the rainforests.

"There are so many ways to care about life. When I know that my actions have made others' lives wonderful, I get a surge of energy. I call that energy GIRAFFE JUICE. It's a magical energy that juices me up and makes me feel alive.

"Sometimes it tingles happily like a jolt of electricity. Sometimes it flows steadily through me, making me feel warm and wonderful… but whatever this energy is, it gives me the power to go out and keep helping others."

"Speaking of helping others..." Eva dipped her hand into her pocket and pulled out a big bandage. She smiled. "I thought you might need a new one for the cut on your leg." Marvel placed his front hoof delicately in Eva's hands.

Eva had a big sunny smile on her face for the entire time she was wrapping the bandage around Marvel's leg.

"I'm not sure I get what you were just saying, Marvel. Are you saying that because I'm alive, I naturally want to

GIRAFFES SAY:

GIRAFFE JUICE is a powerful energy that bubbles up inside of us when we know that we have made life wonderful for ourselves or others.

take care of life? I like that idea. It's almost as if I'm in the same family as all living things...because we're all alive."

When Eva looked up, she noticed that Marvel was looking at her gratefully. She stopped and stared...and then her eyes got wild with delight. "I FEEL IT, MARVEL!"

"What, Eva?"

"The juice, Marvel! I FEEL GIRAFFE JUICE! The whole time I was helping you with your cut I had a warm happy feeling. Then when you looked at me as if to say thank you, I felt a spark of joy fill my heart. It was a bubbly, sparkly kind of excitement that felt good inside of me. How cool is that!"

Eva cut the end of the bandage.

"That must be THE SECRET, Marvel! IT'S GIRAFFE JUICE! It's the good feeling I get when I know that I've helped someone. So when I help others, it helps me too."

Eva stuttered in her excitement, "I...I think it's the reason I like hanging out with you so much. I can really tell how much you like doing things to make life fun—fun for me, you, and everyone."

"Right on, Eva!" Marvel jumped and swirled his tail in a circle. "And one of the things I do to make life fun for everyone is I try to figure what makes people tick. Do you know what I mean? For example, can you guess why Principal Pickle chooses to be principal?"

"To help kids?" Eva guessed.

Marvel moved closer to Eva. "You never know...maybe he was bullied in school and had a dream of creating a school where kids could feel safe. The point is that if he senses that you really care about his needs and dreams, it's more likely he'll want to work with you."

"I'm still a little nervous. Grown-ups have a way of looking at me as if to say, 'You're just a kid; you don't know anything.' One of the reasons I love talking to you is that you seem to really believe in me."

Just then, there was a voice in the distance. "Eva!"

"Oh, that's Ike. It's time to meet with the zoo board members. Wish me luck."

"Good luck, Eva."

~ 23 ~
COMMON GROUND

Marvel kept a watchful eye on the office door, waiting eagerly for Eva, Bo and Ike to emerge. More than an hour passed and Marvel felt a bit anxious.

Suddenly Eva appeared, running full speed in his direction with a big smile on her face. Bo and Ike were close behind her, carrying signs saying "Marvel MATTERS" in gold and brown letters. Eva was the first to reach Marvel's cage.

"You won't believe it, Marvel! The zoo board

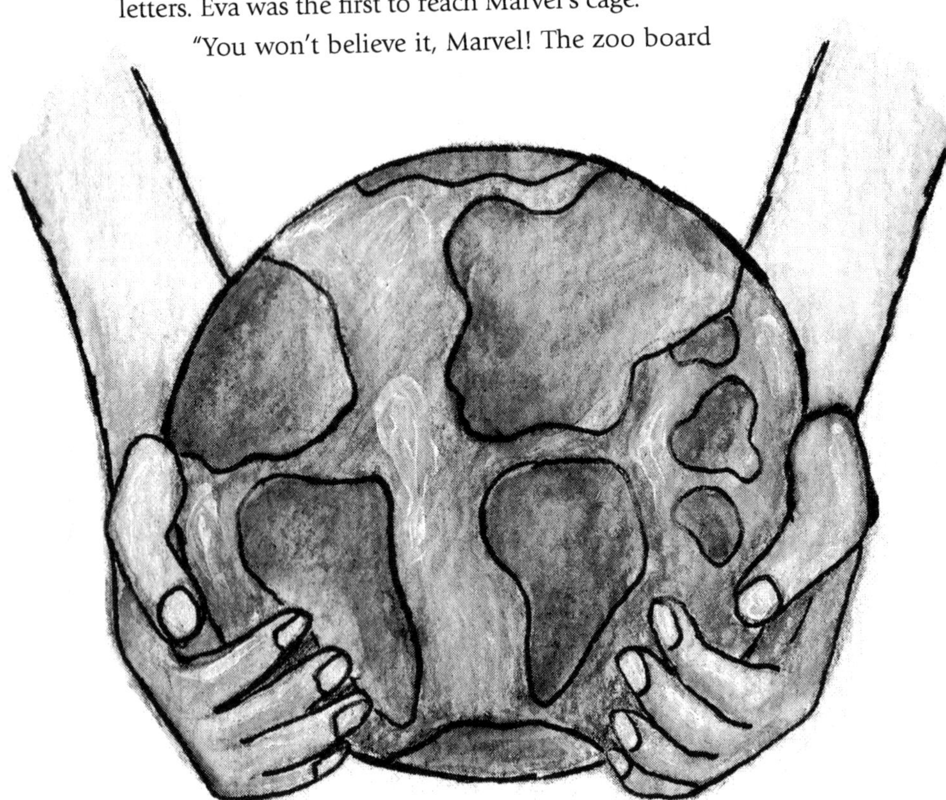

is making plans that will help reunite you with your mom!"

"What happened?" he asked with anticipation.

"Well, when we walked into the meeting—" as Eva spoke, her hands excitedly danced along with her words "—we saw two board members fighting. Bo, Ike and I sat down, and we were feeling pretty uncomfortable.

"One of them called the other one greedy. I spoke up and made a guess about her needs. By the way, I really had no idea. But I remembered you told me to just guess and it worked!"

"Way to go, Eva!" Marvel said proudly.

Eva clasped her hands in front of herself and gave a little shake with her shoulders.

Bo interjected, "Eva was so great, Marvel! How she talked to them really worked!"

"So anyway," Eva got back to the story, "the lady said that she originally got involved with the zoo because she thought it was a great way to inspire people to respect nature. She believes that the more people have an opportunity to fall in love with animals, the more they'll want to protect the wild environments they live in.

"She wants people to understand that every living thing is special and different, and that life is like a magical wizard that has painted the most amazing world ever. Think about all the animals with their incredible colors and the special ways they care for their babies. Think about how every living thing on the planet has its own special way to survive...like how bats use radar..."

"Or the way polar bears can swim in the freezing ocean for miles and miles!" added Ike.

Eva nodded excitedly and continued, "Life has created a total fantasy world...but this fantasy world is real...and what really amazes me is to think about what's giving life its power underneath this magic show...

"I guess that's another story, Marvel, but the point is...This woman on the zoo board wants to use some of the zoo's money to help fund national parks that will allow animals to live freely. She also wants

people to stop polluting the environment because it's causing millions of living things to die. She's even afraid that the whole human race could soon go extinct if we don't learn to live in harmony with the natural world that keeps us alive."

"Wow," Marvel sighed. "I feel relieved knowing that someone on the zoo board cares about the environment in this way."

"And get this." Eva had more to tell him. "The guy she called greedy said he cares about the same things but he also wants to make sure the zoo keeps making money. He doesn't want the zoo to go bankrupt. The two of them stopped arguing, because they started to realize that they both cared about the same things! Just like you taught me!"

Then Ike took over from where Eva left off, "Then another board member spoke up and said that she heard that zoos with safaris were making more money. Do you know what a safari is? It's a fenced-in area with lots of different animals living together and it provides more space for the animals to move around...

"Anyway, it turns out that the same people who own this zoo also own the zoo that's holding your mom! They're planning to start building the safari within a month and you and your mom will be living together there. Can you believe it?"

"I'm delighted," Marvel said with a big fuzzy giraffe smile.

"Us too!" Eva, Bo and Ike said at the same time, before breaking out in laughter.

"It was awesome to see how talking about needs helped everybody find a common ground to care for one another," added Ike.

"Oh, and guess what? Bo's off the hook!" Eva said as she high-fived her beaming brother.

"Yeah, I volunteered to help out at the zoo on weekends so they're not going to press charges!" exclaimed Bo. "I'm psyched because I'll be able to learn more about animals and how to take care of them."

Marvel's ears were wiggling more wildly than ever...and Eva was glowing. She felt strong and proud and then —**BAM!**

It hit her with a blasting force as strong as a volcano. **GIRAFFE JUICE!**

"Do you want to hear my new goal, Marvel?"

"I'd love to," he said, bucking up his front legs like a horse.

"I really want to figure out a way to raise enough money to buy you and your mom from the zoo and set you free. Would you like that?"

"I'm not sure, Eva," Marvel hesitated. "I'm touched that you would want to help me, but because I grew up in a zoo, I'm not sure if I'd be able to survive in the wild."

"You know, I was afraid of that. It reminds me of something that's been bothering me. I was reading up on the Internet last night and I felt confused about whether I believe zoos are really helping animals.

"Zoos say they're hoping to teach people to love animals so that they will want to protect them from going extinct in the wild. But I wonder if they're teaching people the opposite without realizing it."

"What do you mean, Eva?"

"Well, I read a story about the destruction of the rainforests, polluted oceans and the way entire forests in Alaska and throughout the world are just dying off. I couldn't believe it when I read that another species of life goes extinct on this planet every single minute of every day.

"Even life forms that were here before the dinosaurs are disappearing, never to return. And it seems like one of the reasons we have so many problems is that people have been trying to rule over Nature instead of working in harmony with her.

"I wonder if, when people go to the zoo and see the way humans rule over animals, they start to think that it's okay for people to be the rulers over the Earth. It seems to me that this may be one of the reasons for all the problems with the environment today.

"People are trying to rule Nature, to rule other people through war--and even to rule kids! And then kids try to rule over other kids by bullying. I don't know if this makes sense..."

Marvel nodded to Eva and told her silently, through his soft giraffe eyes, that he understood.

Eva went on, "I hope Principal Pickle approves the Giraffe Club, so that kids will stop fighting so much and start figuring out ways to help each other."

Eva looked at her watch, "Oh, slime berries! I told my mom I'd meet her at three. I'll come back and visit you as soon as I can. Okay, Marvel?"

"I'm not going anywhere," Marvel said with a quirky smile. "Oh, and I have something for you." Marvel pushed a small note out from under his cage with his front hoof and said, "Keep this note with you and read it only after the meeting with Principal Pickle. Will you do that?"

It was a tightly folded piece of lime-green paper. Eva, Bo and Ike were burning with curiosity. Still, she promised to wait as patiently as possible to discover the contents of this mysterious message.

~ 24 ~
BUTTERFLIES AND BULLIES

On Monday afternoon, Eva waited for Ike in front of the school. She played with the zipper on her hooded sweatshirt while thinking about the big upcoming meeting with Principal Pickle. Then something caught her eye.

Jip Jackal's mom was at her van with Jip's little brother, trying to get the toddler into his car seat. Mrs. Jackal grabbed him forcefully by the wrist and he began to cry.

Eva wondered whether kids could be learning to bully from the way adults sometimes boss kids around. She thought about how kids could get the idea that it's okay to overpower someone smaller when they see parents use force with their children.

To reduce violence in schools, she wished teachers and parents could learn Giraffe Language instead of overpowering kids with punishments and rewards. Maybe even Jip and his friends could find other ways to express themselves, she thought. Marvel had helped her realize that people could work together in a very different way.

Finally, Ike arrived. They hurried into Principal Pickle's office. Patty was on the phone, as usual. She chirped, "I gotta go, honey," and hung up. Shuffling her papers around, she tried to make it look like she was busy working. "Have a seat, you two. The principal will be with you shortly."

Ike moved closer to Eva and whispered, "I want you to do all the talking." His green hair stood straight up on end.

Eva could tell that Ike needed empathy and she remembered that Marvel told her that sometimes the easiest way is to just listen silently and focus on the other person's needs. Eva looked deeply into Ike's eyes without talking. She wondered if Ike had a need for respect and if he wasn't trusting that Principal Pickle would take him seriously.

Ike breathed a deep sigh of relief and then leaned over and whispered, "I can tell you understand me, Eva."

Just then, Principal Pickle burst forth from behind his office door and said, "Come on in, kids."

Eva and Ike looked at each other as if they were about to get on the scariest roller coaster on Earth.

Butterflies fluttered in Eva's stomach as she followed Ike into the office. She mentally strapped on her giraffe ears—nice and tight!

The moment Principal Pickle closed the office door behind them, he blurted, "Let me be blunt, kids. I read your letter about starting an after-school Giraffe Club. I know you have wonderful intentions, but it's not going to work here at this school. We are already over budget and we just don't have the money to pay for an after-school teacher."

Eva's mind went blank and she couldn't remember anything she'd planned to say. "Umm..."

Principal Pickle was pacing back and forth. "What's the matter? Has the cat got your tongue? I don't want to rush you, but I'm actually very busy today."

Ike just sat there with his mouth open, staring at Eva as if he had seen a ghost.

Eva remembered Marvel's suggestion to find it in her heart to sincerely care about Principal Pickle's needs. Her ears wiggled. "Sounds like you're feeling pressure to get some important things done today, and I'm wondering if you'd prefer to talk on a different day?"

Principal Pickle sat down and his face softened, "Yes, as a principal there are lots of things I want to get done, but I want to talk with you about your request.

"As far as this Giraffe Club you want, I wish I could tell you differently, but there's just nothing to talk about. A Giraffe Club simply won't work here. Like I said, I think it's a great idea, and I commend your efforts, but I regret that the bullying problems we have in our school are a little too complicated for a solution this simple."

Eva wanted to argue, but then she thought again about Marvel's guidance to continue connecting with Principal Pickle's feelings and needs. But what were his feelings and needs? She didn't know. Oh yeah, Marvel told her to just guess. "Principal Pickle, are you feeling concerned for the safety of the students?"

"That's right, Eva. So you can understand how it doesn't make sense to put Jip and all the biggest bullies in the school together in one room and expect there to be anything but trouble."

Eva's ears wiggled in overdrive. "So when you think about Jip and his friends together in the same room, it sounds like you're feeling concerned for everyone's safety."

"Exactly. I'm so glad you understand. I wish I could help you kids, but these big problems really need to be handled by adults."

For a moment, Eva felt angry. It seemed to her that the adults were the ones causing most of the problems. When was the last time a bunch of kids banded together and started a war? ***NEVER!***

She took a breath and gave herself some empathy. Silently, she thought about what she was feeling and needing: She felt upset because her need for respect wasn't met when Principal Pickle said that these problems needed to be handled by adults. She really wanted to tell him he was wrong, but she thought it might affect her chance of connecting with him. So she turned her attention back to trying to figure out what his needs were.

"Principal Pickle, would you like some understanding for just how challenging it can be to work with kids like Jip?"

"Yes," he said softly. "It's tough trying to figure out the right way to guide kids like Jip Jackal. Kids like that need to be taught discipline if they're going to survive in this world."

"It sounds like you really care about Jip and his friends."

Principal Pickle choked on a few words. He paused and stared deeply into the wall behind them, his mind seemingly transported somewhere else. Tears came to his eyes, and then he collected himself.

"Ahh, umm, ahh...I really do care. I care about all the students here. And it's a hard job to try to make everyone happy."

He looked directly into Eva's eyes and said, "The truth is that before this meeting I thought there was no way the Giraffe Club would work, but after this little talk, I may consider it for the future." He glanced at the clock and continued.

"I really need to get a few things done, so maybe we can get back to this at the beginning of the next school year."

Principal Pickle got up from his desk and opened his office door, motioning for Ike and Eva to leave.

Eva felt distraught and confused. Next school year! That seemed like an eternity. She wasn't sure if she should begin to argue her point or what. Then, out of nowhere, they heard Patty squeal, "Excuse me! JIP!"

Jip came busting loudly and recklessly into the office, completely uninvited. Everyone froze.

~ 25 ~
WHO LET THE CAT OUT OF THE BAG?

Jip put his hands on his hips, like a superhero, and announced, "I heard through the grapevine that you were having a meeting about a Giraffe Club and I have something to say about it!"

Principal Pickle started to say, "Now Jip, if you think..."

Jip interrupted and declared, "I think a Giraffe Club is a great idea!"

Eva and Ike looked at each other in amazement and total confusion. How did he hear about the Giraffe Club? And how did he know about this meeting? They squinted at one another, each wondering if the other had let the cat out of the bag. *Didn't we agree this was top secret?*

Principal Pickle spoke up. "Our meeting is over, and we've decided to consider the idea for the beginning of school next year."

Jip replied, "I think it would be best for everyone if we get it started as soon as possible. Why don't we get the Giraffe Club started next Monday?"

Principal Pickle looked stunned for a moment, and then his face changed. He stiffened his upper lip and said, "You can't fool me. You and your buddies are just looking for a new way to cause trouble."

Ike and Eva still couldn't believe this was happening. But then the unthinkable happened...Jip's ears started to wiggle. His eyes and face became soft, and he said, "Principal Pickle, are you feeling concerned that my buddies and I won't respect the school rules?"

"You're darned right I am! If you want me to be quite honest, you and your buddies have wasted more of my time this year than I can ever remember in my entire career as a principal."

Jip's ears were wiggling wildly! "It sounds like you're really frustrated about how hard it's been for you to do your job this year and you're wishing things could be easier."

Principal Pickle raised his voice even more. "And I'm feeling angry, because nothing I do seems to be helping!"

Ike and Eva held their breath.

"Jip, I know we've had a hard year, but I really care about you and your future. I don't know how to help you and I've almost given up trying."

There was complete silence in the room. Jip's ears continued to wiggle. "I'm hearing you say you really care about me and you're feeling hopeless about how to help me."

"That's right." Principal Pickle paused and bit his lip. "I feel so relieved hearing you say that, Jip. All this time I've thought that you believed I was out to get you. It would bring me a lot of happiness to be able to help you."

Jip's ears were wiggling like crazy, but this time instead of speaking, he took in Principal Pickle's words in silence. Then he lowered his head. His eyes welled up and a teardrop streaked down the side of his face.

Eva, Ike and Principal Pickle looked at each other as if they were witnessing a miracle. After a long silence, Jip looked up at Principal Pickle and said, "After hearing everything you've said, I feel sad and confused about why I've had such a hard time showing people how much I like them. But I'm starting to learn new ways."

Principal Pickle put his hand on his heart. "I feel relieved and amazed to hear you say these things. Is this the Giraffe Communication stuff that Eva and Ike have been telling me about?"

Jip nodded.

"Interesting." Principal Pickle shut the office door and then closed his eyes so tightly that his forehead got all crinkled up.

"I'll tell you what, kids. We can try the club for one month, and if it goes well, maybe we can continue. If I have any problems with you or your buddies, Jip, I'm canceling the project.

"I'll supervise. That way I won't have to spend money hiring an after-school teacher and I can make sure no one gets hurt. Besides, I might want to learn how to use some of this Giraffe Language to get along better with my staff. We can start next Monday. How does that sound?"

Jip slapped Eva a high-five, "AWESOME!"

Eva wasn't quite finished. "Principal Pickle, I understand that you'd like to supervise and look after everyone's safety, but I would like the kids to be running the meetings. Is that cool with you?"

With a sincere smile on his face, he said, "Okay, done. Now get out of here so I can get back to my business."

The three of them jumped for joy as they stepped into the hallway. Eva couldn't wipe the smile off of her face. It suddenly felt like she had her old friend back.

Eva grabbed Jip by both shoulders and whispered, "You did it! How on Earth…?"

Ike was jumping up and down chanting "Giraffe Club! Giraffe Club!"

Jip grinned. "After talking with Marvel, I realized it's not actually that much fun to pick on people all the time."

Eva's breath got caught somewhere inside of her chest. *Could this be for real? Could Jip really have changed so quickly?* And then she remembered how her heart changed towards her brother, her parents and even Principal Pickle after talking with Marvel. And then she believed it. Jip had learned Giraffe Language!

"When did you talk to him?" Eva asked, surprised.

"Remember Saturday when you were at the zoo? I was spying on you, and I thought you had lost your mind talking to a giraffe. After you left, I went over to see what the heck was going on. Then I heard a weird deep voice that said, 'Hi. My name is Marvel.' I looked around, figuring someone was in the bushes playing a prank on me.

"When I told him my name, he said that he'd heard about me through you guys. I was expecting him to get on my case for bullying, like everyone else. But instead he just listened to me for a while.

"It was weird, but the more I talked to him, the better I felt about myself. He seemed to understand me and accept me the way I am. No one has ever asked me such strange questions about my needs.

"I kept expecting him to do what people always do to me—act nice for a little while and then tell me why my behavior is unacceptable. But he didn't do that! He just listened.

"By the end of the conversation, I asked him if he would teach me to talk and listen to people the way he did. He told me to come back the next day for a crash course. So after Sunday School, I went to the zoo. That's when I found out about the Giraffe Club and your meeting with Principal Pickle."

The three of them walked together through the hall, and then out the door to the playground. Once outside, Eva felt inspired to reach into her pocket for her harmonica. She breathed life into the little instrument and a joyful song blasted through the air. Ike and Jip bobbed their heads in rhythm with Eva's music—the universal language of music casting a sense of peace over the three of the them.

"I loved that song," Jip said with a soft shy voice as Eva put the harmonica back into her pocket.

"Thanks," Eva shrugged in her own shy way.

"And," Jip put his fist up to his mouth as he cleared his throat, "I also really like," he nervously cleared his throat again, "well, I also think your guitar playing is really cool." He dropped his head so Eva couldn't see his eyes.

"I feel bummed that I said those things to you after the talent show that day. I don't know why I said that when the truth is...I wish I could play like you. I've sort of missed hanging out with you and listening to you play your guitar."

He lifted his head to peek at Eva's expression. She was smiling. He smiled back. "So you think maybe you could teach me how to play guitar some day?"

"Well," Eva looked down to the ground as she admitted, "I sort of miss hanging out with you and laughing at your jokes."

"Okay!" Ike's voice chimed in, reminding them that he was there too. "How about if Eva teaches you to play guitar, Jip, and in return, you get back to telling Eva your jokes again! Does that sound like a deal?"

"Deal!" Eva exclaimed.

"Deal!" Jip stuck out his hand and they did the secret handshake they made up from back in the days when they used to run around as friends.

Eva stood there in disbelief. She was overwhelmed with a mixture of joy and sorrow for how much she had missed being friends with Jip. Feeling a little embarrassed because she was about to cry, she hugged Jip with all her might.

Then tears of joy started pouring from her eyes. She knew that all the pain of the last couple of years probably would never have happened if they had met Marvel sooner.

Gratitude welled up in Eva's heart and filled her whole body with tingles. This was a real-life dream come true!

~ 26 ~
ANYTHING IS POSSIBLE!

Suddenly, like a lightning bolt up their spines, all three of them felt a power that they had never felt before.

Eva looked Jip squarely in the eyes with a clear and intense focus. "I'm still amazed that we convinced Principal Pickle that quickly! If we could do that, then anything is possible! I wonder if other kids would like to learn Giraffe Language so they could talk to teachers about how they can make school more fun.

Jip was stoked, "And if Giraffe Club is cool, maybe kids at other schools would want to do it too. And we could help them get started. That way kids...and even, parents and teachers...could learn a new way to get along if they want to!"

Ike chimed in, "I just joined an after school club that has a goal of planting a hundred fruit trees in the next month…so it's good for the environment, and there will be yummy food for people to eat too. Maybe in the Giraffe Club we could come up with some ideas like this so we can practice working together as teammates."

"Yeah! And we can play all sorts of games!" Eva said "And we can get giraffe ears and jackal ears to wear so we can have fun practicing Giraffe Language."

"Jackal ears?" Jip looked confused wondering what his last name had to do with it.

Eva gave a little giggle. "I'll explain later."

Just then, Eva remembered Marvel's mysterious note. She quickly pulled it out of her pocket and read it aloud to Ike and Jip:

Dear Eva,

I know that many people throughout the world have lost hope, but now you understand why my faith in humanity is so strong. When people choose to sincerely care about one another, there's no need for violence. Things just seem to magically work themselves out... oftentimes in surprising and unexpected ways.

When the human heart is full of compassion... ANYTHING IS POSSIBLE!

Say hi to Jip and Ike for me.

See you soon,

Marvel

Giraffe
CLUB

www.GiraffeJuice.com

Would you take action if you knew that your effort could significantly decrease violence in the lives of young people? What if it was easy, took around a minute of your time, and was free?

REQUEST: Please go to www.GiraffeJuice.com/share and share the first 2 chapters of the full-color e-book of *Giraffe Juice* with anyone whom you think would appreciate receiving it. It's free and will take less than a minute.

You'll be taking part in using the power of media and the Internet to spread the awareness of Nonviolent Communication around the world! Over time, your single action sharing this book, could result in hundreds...even thousands... of people becoming exposed to Nonviolent Communication (NVC) for the first time...REALLY!

Our vision is to distribute a million copies of *Giraffe Juice* to kids and adults throughout the world, in either its physical or e-book form, by January 1st 2012.

THE MILLION GIRAFFES PROJECT IS ON THE GO!

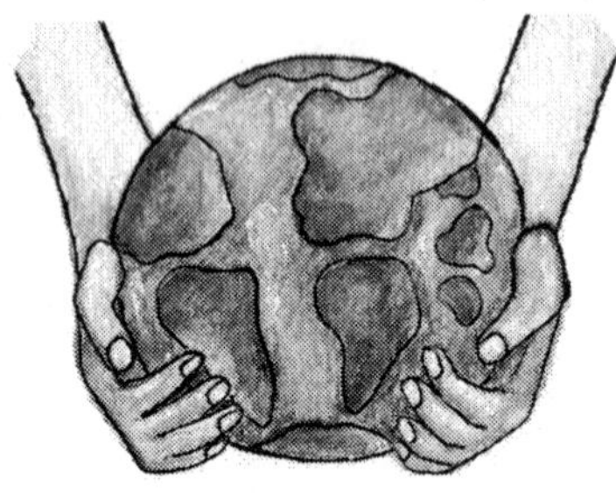

We have acquired charitable donations for the nonprofit distribution of *Giraffe Juice* to schools, libraries, and organizations all over the globe. Our intention is to participate in co-creating a planet where people are increasingly able to experience peace within themselves, their families, and in the world.

Knowing that there are big people and little people who shy away from academic approaches to learning, one of the intentions of *Giraffe Juice* is to share a fun and entertaining entryway into the heart of Giraffe Language. Its goal is not to teach Nonviolent Communication, but rather to offer a whimsical glimpse into the spirit of the work so anyone may choose to learn more if they feel inspired.

Is there a teacher, parent, or young person you would enjoy sharing this book with?

Would you enjoy knowing that your choice to share the free e-book with someone you care about inspired this person to begin practicing Nonviolent Communication with his or her family, school, or organization?

If yes, go to www.GiraffeJuice.com/share and we'll show you how to spread the word. It's easy.

Ninety percent of the proceeds from the sale of the physical book (at www.GiraffeJuice.com) will be allocated to spreading Giraffe Language throughout the world via the Million Giraffes Project. The remaining ten percent will be donated to the Center for Nonviolent Communication to support its social change and peace-making efforts.

The Million Giraffes Project will be posting its progress regularly so you can keep tabs on how quickly we are achieving our goals. If you feel inspired to support this project through service see next page for more clarity. If you wish to make a charitable donation you can contact JP directly at: jp@GiraffeJuice.com.

www.GiraffeJuice.com

ARE YOU A PARENT OR A TEACHER NEEDING SUPPORT?

At www.GiraffeJuice.com you will find:

- Parent/teacher forums where you can connect with others and request support
- Youth forums where youth can support one another to grow their giraffe language skills
- Info about giraffe schools/camps
- A complete learning guide of NVC books, videos, CD's, and other resources

PLEASE COME AND POST YOUR PROJECT ON GIRAFFEJUICE.COM!

At GiraffeJuice.com you will be able to easily post any NVC-related projects, resources or individual missions that you would like to share with others. You are also welcomed to post projects and resources not specific to NVC, if you are confident they will support parents, teachers, and kids in deepening their Giraffe skills.

WOULD YOU ENJOY CO-CREATING THE SEQUEL?

We're already planning the sequel to *Giraffe Juice* to better serve its mission in the world...if you are a best-selling author or editor of kids' books and are very confident with your NVC skills, we would love to work with you. We're also looking to hire highly experienced professionals with the following skills: developmental editing, plot development, web development, marketing, and workbook development (please respond only if you feel extremely confident with your NVC skills). Contact jp@giraffejuice.com.

THE MILLION GIRAFFES PROJECT WOULD LOVE YOUR SUPPORT.

If you feel uneasy about your Giraffe skills, there are still many ways to contribute. Firstly, e-mailing the link for the first chapters of the e-book of *Giraffe Juice* to as many people as possible will be an enormous contribution. Secondly, we would love to hire people with the following skills: project management, web design, marketing, distribution, proofreading, voiceover (for the audio book), music, visual art, graphic art, and school administration. If you're interested in connecting with us, or making a charitable donation, write to jp@GiraffeJuice.com.

www.GiraffeJuice.com

At GiraffeJuice.com you can:

- **Instantly share access to the full-color e-book of *Giraffe Juice* with someone you care about (for free).**
- Purchase a physical copy of this book or its companion workbook.
  The *Giraffe Juice Workbook* is a super-fun way for young people, and others young at heart, to deepen their Giraffe skills. (Significant discounts available for the purchase of multiple copies.)

At www.GiraffeJuice.com you can also find out how to get:

- Giraffe games, puppets, and ears.

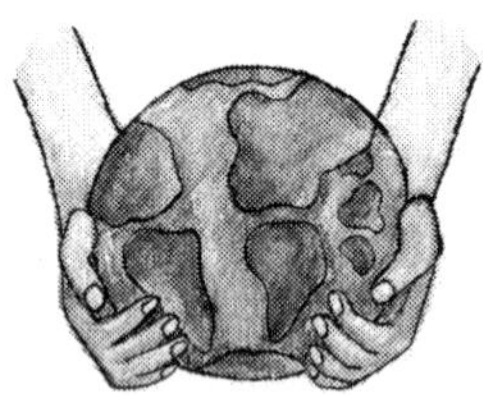

NVC Resources For Kids, Parents and Educators

In the upcoming pages you will find a list of books, games, and other fun stuff to help young people and adults deepen their giraffe skills. This resource guide is focused on supporting the use of Nonviolent Communication (NVC) with young people and does not include works that are intended solely for adults. Our intention is to offer you a broad range of choices while acknowledging the sincere efforts of giraffe authors, trainers, and teachers worldwide. Though we do endorse the large majority of what you will find below, we have not reviewed all of these recommendations (so, please consider doing a bit of your own research).

If you would like to submit a resource to be included in the next edition of *Giraffe Juice*, e-mail JP Allen at jp@giraffejuice.com. Because www.GiraffeJuice.com is updated frequently, your submission will be promptly added to the online resource.

NVC Resources for Young People

Charlie and Sophie series of nine picture books
by Vilma Costetti
Paperback: (32 pp.)
http://heartvistas.com/books.aspx

Ginny Be a Good Frog
by Vilma Costetti
Paperback: (23 pp.)
www.cnvc.org/en/bookstore/cnvc-store-printed-items (order#: nvc0508)

Lilla känsloboken (Swedish)
Little Book of Feelings (English)
Väike Tunneteraamat (Estonian)
by Liv Larsson and Maria Tison-Larsson
Paperback: (90 pp.) Currently available in Swedish and Estonian only.
http://friareliv.se/index.php/en/books-about-nvc/children-books/215-lilla-kaensloboken

The Mayor of Jackal Heights
by Rita Herzog & Kathy Smith
Paperback: (28 pp.)
www.cnvc.org/en/bookstore/cnvc-store-printed-items (order#: nvc105)

Kids Eye-View of Speaking Compassion DVD
Speaking Compassion NVC Basic Training DVD
Kids Eye-View of Speaking Compassion DVD
Practice Practice Practice! An illustrated study guide
Games for Speaking Compassion K-8 gamebook
by Holley Humphrey
http://empathymagic.com/index.php?cid=321

Zak
by Bridget Belgrave
Paperback: (160 pp.)
http://heartvistas.com/books.aspx

Feeleez
by Kris Laroche, Nathan McTague, and Natalie Christensen
Card game, buttons, and poster featuring illustrated images to help children develop emotional vocabulary.
www.feeleez.com

NVC Resources for Parents

Connected Parenting
by Inbal Kashtan
Compact disk:
www.baynvc.org/connected_parenting_cd.php

Parenting From Your Heart:
Sharing the Gifts of Compassion, Connection and Choice
by Inbal Kashtan
Paperback: (48 pp.)
http://nonviolentcommunication.com/store/product_info.php?products_id=39
E-book:
http://nonviolentcommunication.com/store/product_info.php?products_id=112

Parenting with Nonviolent Communication by Inbal Kashtan
YouTube video (8:15):
www.youtube.com/watch?v=IQO7h9MNCqI

Raising Children Compassionately:
Parenting the Nonviolent Communication Way
by Marshall B. Rosenberg, Ph.D.
Paperback: (32 pp.)
http://nonviolentcommunication.com/store/product_info.php?products_id=32
E-book:
http://nonviolentcommunication.com/store/product_info.php?products_id=67

Connection Parenting: Parenting through Connection instead of Coercion, Through Love instead of Fear
by Pam Leo
Paperback: (216 pp.)
www.amazon.com/exec/obidos/ASIN/1932279768/pamleoconnepa-20

Growing Up in Trust: Raising Kids Without Rewards
by Justine Mol
Paperback: (144 pp.)
www.amazon.com/Growing-Up-Trust-Justine-Mol/dp/1846941059

Respectful Parents, Respectful Kids:
7 Keys to Turn Family Conflicts into Cooperation
by Sura Hart and Victoria Kindle Hodson
Paperback: (252 pp.)
http://nonviolentcommunication.com/store/product_info.php?products_id=48
E-book:
http://nonviolentcommunication.com/store/product_info.php?products_id=84

Parenting teleclasses
by Ingrid Bauer
NVC Academy (plus other long-distance learning opportunities)
http://nvctraining.com (choose Our Programs > Telecourses)
Read a description of Ingrid's telecourse here:
http://nvctraining.com/courses/telecourses/IB/parenting-practice-popup.html

NVC online article archive for parenting and families:
www.nonviolentcommunication.com/aboutnvc/article_archive.htm#Parenting

NVC resources for parents
(a listing from the Center for Nonviolent Communication):
www.cnvc.org

NVC Yahoo! Group
(online discussion group for parents):
http://groups.yahoo.com/group/nvc-parenting/

Compassionate Parenting Weekly Tips Series (free weekly e-mail tips):
www.nonviolentcommunication.com/parenting_tips/

Connection Times: Creating Thriving Personal and Professional Relationships (a monthly NVC-based newsletter intended to help you transform conflicts, tensions and adversarial relationships and create genuine human connection in every area of your life.) The topics vary from issue to issue and include couples relationships, workplace, parenting, relationships with family members and others.
www.ConnectionTimes.org

Parent Peer Leadership Program (BayNVC, California USA)
Annual program for parents who want to share NVC with parents in their communities:
www.baynvc.org/pplp.php

NVC Resources for Educators

Life-Enriching Education: Help Schools Improve Performance, Reduce Conflict and Enhance Relationships by Marshall B. Rosenberg, Ph.D.
Paperback: (192 pp.)
http://nonviolentcommunication.com/store/product_info.php?products_id=33

The Compassionate Classroom: Relationship Based Teaching and Learning by Sura Hart and Victoria Kindle Hodson
Paperback: (208 pp.)
http://nonviolentcommunication.com/store/product_info.php?products_id=34

The Giraffe Classroom: Where Teaching is a Pleasure and Learning is a Joy by Nancy Sokol Green
Spiral bound: (122 pp.)
www.cnvc.org/en/bookstore/cnvc-store-printed-items (order#: nvc104)

The No-Fault Classroom: Tools to Resolve Conflict & Foster Relationship Intelligence by Sura Hart and Victoria Kindle Hodson
Paperback: (256 pp.)
http://nonviolentcommunication.com/store/product_info.php?products_id=105
E-book:
http://nonviolentcommunication.com/store/product_info.php?products_id=113

Teaching Children Compassionately: How Students and Teachers Can Succeed with Mutual Understanding by Marshall B. Rosenberg, Ph.D.
Paperback: (48 pp.)
http://nonviolentcommunication.com/store/product_info.php?products_id=41

Heart Talk for Kids—NVC-based educational curriculum
(pre-K through 6th grade) by Veronica Lassen and Debbie Grieb
16 lessons on compact disk:
http://heartvistas.com/nvccurriculum.aspx

Transforming Power Relations: The Invisible Revolution by Miki Kashtan
Article in Encounter: Education for Meaning and Social Justice, Volume 15, Number 3, Autumn 2002 (This issue contains additional NVC content.)
www.great-ideas.org/enc.htm

Additional NVC Resources

Communication FUNdamentals by Jean Morrison and Christine King
Paperback: (56 pp.)
www.nvcproducts.com

GROK Cards by Jean Morrison and Christine King
15 games for all ages, using feelings and needs cards.
(GROK Kids version in development).
www.nvcproducts.com

Ich will verstehen, was du wirklich brauchst: Gewaltfreie Kommunikation mit Kindern—Das Projekt Giraffentraum
(German)
I Want to Understand What You Really Need: Nonviolent Communication with Children—The Project Giraffentraum
(English)—not yet available
by Frank and Gundi Gaschler
Paperback: (140 pp.) Currently available in German and Korean only.
Amazon: http://www.amazon.de
Information: http://www.giraffentraum.de/

Magnetic GROK by Jean Morrison and Christine King
Magnetic feeling, need, and phrase words for use on metal surfaces.
www.nvcproducts.com

The No-Fault Zone Game by Sura Hart and Victoria Kindle Hodson
Ages 5 and up:
www.k-hcommunication.com/games.html

Restorative Circles
A safe, inclusive, creative space for having and learning from conflict.
Currently being used in Brazilian and North American schools and families (among other applications).
Write Dominic Barter at contact@restorativecircles.org for more information.

INTERNATIONAL CENTER FOR NONVIOLENT COMMUNICATION

The Center for Nonviolent Communication (CNVC) is a global organization whose vision is a world where all people are getting their needs met and resolving their conflicts peacefully. In this vision, people are using Nonviolent Communication (NVC, referred to as "Giraffe Language" in this book) to create and participate in networks of worldwide life-serving systems in economics, education, justice, healthcare and peace-keeping.

Nonviolent Communication training evolved from Dr. Marshall Rosenberg's quest to find a way of rapidly disseminating much-needed peacemaking skills. The Center for Nonviolent Communication emerged out of work he was doing with civil rights activists in the early 1960s. During this period, he provided mediation and communication skills training to communities working to peacefully desegregate schools and other public institutions.

Since the center's inception, the response to Nonviolent Communication training has been extremely positive. It is seen as a powerful tool for peacefully resolving differences at personal, professional and political levels.

To learn more, visit www.cnvc.org online.

www.cnvc.org. E-mail: cnvc@cnvc.org
Phone: +1-505-244-4041

FEELINGS

Feelings when your needs are satisfied

AFFECTIONATE
compassionate
friendly
loving
open hearted
sympathetic
tender
warm

CONFIDENT
empowered
open
proud
safe
secure

ENGAGED
absorbed
alert
curious
engrossed
enchanted
entranced
fascinated
interested
intrigued
involved
spellbound
stimulated

INSPIRED
amazed
awed
wonder

EXCITED
amazed
animated
ardent
aroused
astonished
dazzled
eager
energetic
enthusiastic
giddy
invigorated
lively
passionate
surprised
vibrant

EXHILARATED
blissful
ecstatic
elated
enthralled
exuberant
radiant
rapturous
thrilled

GRATEFUL
appreciative
moved
thankful
touched

HOPEFUL
expectant
encouraged
optimistic

JOYFUL
amused
delighted
glad
happy
jubilant
pleased
tickled

PEACEFUL
calm
clear headed
comfortable
centered
content
equanimous
fulfilled
mellow
quiet
relaxed
relieved
satisfied
serene
still
tranquil
trusting

REFRESHED
enlivened
rejuvenated
renewed
rested
restored
revived

FEELINGS

Feelings when your needs are not satisfied

CONFUSED
ambivalent
baffled
bewildered
dazed
hesitant
lost
mystified
perplexed
puzzled
torn

TENSE
anxious
cranky
distressed
distraught
edgy
fidgety
frazzled
irritable
jittery
nervous
overwhelmed
restless
stressed out

DISCONNECTED
alienated
aloof
apathetic
bored
cold
detached
distant
distracted
indifferent
numb
removed
uninterested
withdrawn
gloomy
heavy hearted
hopeless
melancholy
unhappy
wretched

FATIGUED
beat
burnt out
depleted
exhausted
lethargic
listless
sleepy
tired
weary
worn out

VULNERABLE
fragile
guarded
helpless
insecure
leery
reserved
sensitive
shaky

YEARNING
envious
jealous
longing
nostalgic
pining
wistful

EMBARRASSED
ashamed
chagrined
flustered
guilty
mortified
self-conscious

FEELINGS

Feelings when your needs are not satisfied

AFRAID
apprehensive
dread
foreboding
frightened
mistrustful
panicked
petrified
scared
suspicious
terrified
wary
worried

ANNOYED
aggravated
dismayed
disgruntled
displeased
exasperated
frustrated
impatient
irritated
irked

ANGRY
enraged
furious
incensed
indignant
irate
livid
outraged
resentful

PAIN
agony
anguished
bereaved
devastated
grief
heartbroken
hurt
lonely
miserable
regretful
remorseful

SAD
depressed
dejected
despair
despondent
disappointed
discouraged
disheartened
forlorn

AVERSION
animosity
appalled
contempt
disgusted
dislike
hate
horrified
hostile
repulsed

DISQUIET
Agitated
alarmed
discombobulated
disconcerted
disturbed
perturbed
rattled
restless
shocked
startled
surprised
troubled
turbulent
turmoil
uncomfortable
uneasy
unnerved
unsettled
upset

NEEDS

Partial List of Giraffe Needs

CONNECTION
acceptance
affection
appreciation
belonging
cooperation
communication
closeness
community
companionship
compassion
consideration
consistency
empathy
inclusion
intimacy
love
mutuality
nurturing
respect
self-respect
safety
security
stability
support
to know
to be known
to see
to be seen
to understand
to be understood
trust
warmth

AUTONOMY
choice
freedom
independence
space
spontaneity

PHYSICAL
WELL-BEING
air
food
movement
exercise
rest/sleep
sexual expression
safety
shelter
touch
water

MEANING
awareness
celebration of life
challenge
clarity
competence
consciousness
contribution
creativity
discovery
efficacy
effectiveness
growth
hope
learning
mourning
participation
purpose
self-expression
stimulation
to matter
understanding

PEACE
beauty
communion
ease
equality
harmony
inspiration
order

HONESTY
authenticity
integrity
presence

PLAY
joy
humor

MARCI WINTERS

(CO-AUTHOR OF GIRAFFE JUICE)

Marci dedicates *Giraffe Juice* in loving memory of Christian Valentino Arvesen and My Beautiful Grandmas, Helen Gross and Adele Winters

Marci Winters is an educator living on mystical Maui with her Giraffe sweetheart, Shai, and magical cat, Jaya. She is a screenwriter, producer, director and composer.

Her family film, SWEETWATER (www.sweetwaterfilm.com), aired on PBS and is endorsed by KIDS FIRST!: The Coalition for Quality Children's Media. Marci is certified in Yoga, Chi Quong, Mediation and Meditation. She envisions a brighter world, graced with beautiful smiling Giraffes!

Mahalo to Shaikelekuleku, kof gadol sheli, my best friend and brother Jarod Winters and his incredibly supportive, wise wife Par-Par Sonja whose sweetness and love has carried me, The Nettervilles who I am indebted to beyond measure, Jill Stone, your friendship is invaluable, Saundra McKenna, my inspired goddess, Caprice Winneman your heart warms me, Beth Pratt, my faithful friend and Edna and Amir Arbel–for all your yummies!

More Mahlos and Todahs to Talia and Doron "Gamal" Hacham, so many laughs, Nitzan Solomonav, Avi "M'Seba", your yummies too and to Co Co Baldwin, Lesa Sowell, Kathy Doyle, Debbie Siebers, Marni Galef, my soulful sisterhood, Austin, Kauai and Maui Community for your support through soulful sister and brotherhood. JP, all the Allens, and Limor, her beautiful kids for sharing the Giraffe Juice vision..

And to family and friends at the Sivananda Yoga Ashram in Paradise Island, Carmon you opened my inner eye, Norma, Zoey, and all the Levins, Mala, Michael, Maera, Carol, Belle, Ronni, Sarit, Nicole, Mai and Yoav in Israel. And especially to my students everywhere who are all my teachers.

JP ALLEN

(CO-AUTHOR AND PUBLISHER OF GIRAFFE JUICE)

www.KidsHarmonica.com and **www.Harmonica.com/nvc** have enabled JP to share harmonica with people all over world. He delights in helping people play for their own enjoyment as well as developing the skills to play for others.

In Austin, Texas, JP founded Aardvark Music School for kids and taught guitar, drums, piano, song writing, and harmonica. He has a particular love for harmonica because of the ease with which beginners and non-musicians are able to freely express themselves through music.

JP completed pre-medical studies, graduating from Northwestern University in 1988 with a BA in psychology and an enduring interest in educational psychology.

JP has directed several summer camps for kids that focused on sharing music, acting, and peaceful conflict resolution through the process of Nonviolent Communication.

His love for the healing arts is currently expressed through regular practice of Tai Chi, Chi Gong, Yoga, meditation, nourishing whole-foods, and runs on the beach at sunset.

As a professional harmonica player, JP played on CNN, Fox News, and toured the world with Grammy-nominated Abra Moore.

He is currently living on the island of Kauai, Hawaii.

E-mail: jp@GiraffeJuice.com

TAMARA LAPORTE

(ILLUSTRATOR OF GIRAFFE JUICE)

Passionate about nonviolent communication and art, Tamara works as a full time artist and conflict resolution consultant. She co-owns MasonLaporte Conflict Transformation (www.masonlaporte.org), teaches art online over at www.willowing.ning.com, and enjoys making empathy monsters and puppets.

Tamara worked as a drama and art teacher in an international primary school in Sri Lanka for 2.5 years where she wrote and directed her own school play "Whizzbo the Helpful Skweekabee". She deeply believes that peace is possible through self-enquiry, empathy and compassionate communication. At present she lives in Brighton – Hove in England with her partner, the magical Andy. She likes pink bubblegum, avocados, humor and kindness. More of her art can be viewed here: www.willowing.org.

BRITA LIND & TANIA WOLK

(DEVELOPMENTAL EDITOR AND GRAPHIC DESIGNER OF GIRAFFE JUICE)

Brita Lind and Tania Wolk are the co-owners of Go Giraffe Go Writing & Design Inc., an award-winning graphic design and advertising firm.

Brita Lind is a writer and playwright who enjoys living her own dreams and helping others do the same. A believer in, and practitioner of, Nonviolent Communication, Brita believes that NVC holds magical connection and is possible to practice no matter what age we are.

Also a practitioner of NVC, Tania's specialties include working with type so words and thoughts are the stars of the pages and using graphic design to make artists' ideas shine. Tania was tickled pantone #239u (deep pink) to have participated in the NVC Parent Peer Leadership Program (PPLP) in 2006. Part of the Peaceful Families, Peaceful World Project of the International Center for Nonviolent Communication and Bay NVC, PPLP is a learning ground for parents to deepen their NVC practice and to develop the skills to share NVC with other parents.

Go Giraffe Go Writing & Design helps people and organizations do branding and advertising—everything from books and music CD designs...to brochures, websites, logos and advertising campaigns.

Together, Brita and Tania are the moms of two children with whom they share giraffe language as best they can as part of their daily regimen of the heart.

www.GoGiraffeGo.com

ACKNOWLEDGEMENTS

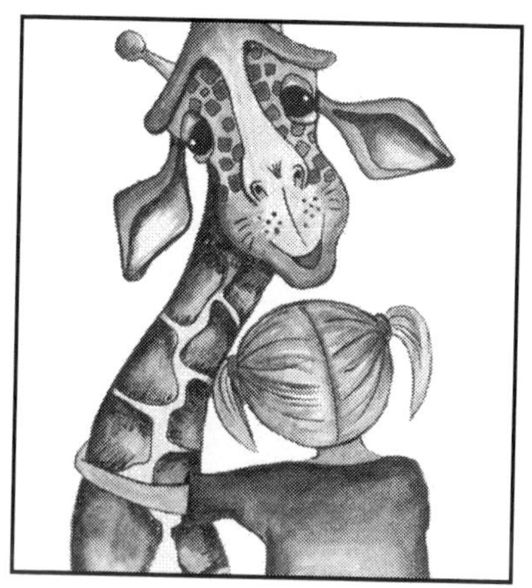

Marci Winters and JP Allen wrote *Giraffe Juice* at the request of Dr. Marshall Rosenberg, founder of the international Center for Nonviolent Communication (CNVC). In addition to the obvious inspiration from Marshall's life work, this book contains many direct transcriptions of dialogues that Marshall created at the 2003 NVC International Intensive Training in Rochester, New York. Thank you Marshall for your loving support of this project. This story is the fulfillment of your request to find new fun ways to share NVC with the world.

The writers and contributors of this book thank you for the path you have laid for living the essence of Nonviolent Communication (NVC). It is a path marked clearly enough for us to see, while encouraging each of us to roam freely in our own unique way.

JP and Marci would like to extend an extra special thank you to Laurie Masters and Candi Sary for bringing a spirit of fun to the words of this book and to Inbal Kashtan for her consistent support of this project.

SPECIAL THANKS TO:

DEVELOPMENTAL EDITORS:

Laurie Masters, Candi Sary, Brita Lind, Jim and Jori Manske, Marshall Rosenberg (dialogue development), Zachary Ossefort

PROOF READERS:

Keith Ely, Pamela D. Pollack

KID EDITORS:

Morgan, Griffin, Drake, and Connor Allen, Aaraaa Aquarian, William S. Johns

JP THANKS:

Diane and Peter Allen, Alan and Janet Winters, Sue Rudolf, Daniel, Ariela, and Olivia Montbriand, Kristen King, Kyra Freestar, Dian Killian, Christa Morph, Inbal Kashtan, Limor Farber (the artist we love who sketched the harmonica player in the "Other Works by the Authors" section at the beginning at the book), Amy Chang, Rosa Russell, Scott Lewis, LaShelle Chardé, Jeff Brown, Joel Heller, Michael Parish, Jessica Vanlandingham, Nadine Helm, Robert Gonzales, Ike Lasater, Sigal Shoham, Rachel Clark, Glenda Mattinson, Blake and Astrid Drolson, Steven, Merlyn and Kalei Ruddell, Sherrie Anderson, Isa Maria, Tewa Holloway, Nick Good, Codi Bear, Rose Miller, Morgan Quinn, and the Creative Spirit and Infinite Wisdom that lives in all of us.

Dalai Lama, Mahatma Gandhi, Mother Teresa, Nelson Mandela, Maya Angelou, Henry David Thoreau, Desmond Tutu, Martin Luther King, Jr., Michael Franti, Eleanor Roosevelt, John Lennon, Yoko Ono, Oprah Winfrey, Marshal Rosenberg, Indira Gandhi, Rosa Parks, William Wilberforce, Jane Goodall, Lach Walesa, Thich Nhat Hanh, Lao Tzu, Harriet Beecher Stowe, Gloria Steinem, Virginia Brown, Princess Diana, Daw Aung San Suu Kyi, Golda Meir, Morihei Ueshiba, Benazir Bhutto, Harry Belafonte, Albert Schweitzer, Riane Eisler, Anderson Sá, Astrid Lindgren, Bruno Hussar, Susan B. Anthony, Anna Reeves Jarvis, Julia Ward Howe, Chiune Sempo Sugihara, Colman McCarthy, Dennis Brutus, Maharishi Mahesh Yogi, Dikembe Mutombo, Ellen Johnson Sirleaf, Greg Smith, Helen Caldicott, Henry Salt, Iqbal Masih, Iris Berben, Joan Baez, Julia Butterfly Hill, Kim Dae Jung, Kujtesa Bejtullahu, Lester Pearson, Paul David Hewson (Bono), Maharishi Mahesh Yogi, Jackson Brown, Eddie Vedder, Martti Ahtisaari, Mary Peters, Mary Therese Winifred Robinson, Nader Khalili, Oscar Arias, Paul Rusesabagina, Rachel Carson, Sabriye Tenberken, Stanley "Tookie" Williams, Sylvia Earle, Vandanna Shiva, Wangari Maathai and...you.

LOVE...COMPASSION.....................................PEACE